FINDING YOU

A Memoir

KRISTEN G. WILLIAMS

Finding You: A Memoir
All Scripture quotations, unless otherwise indicated, are taken from the
Holy Bible, New International Version®, NIV®. Copyright ©1973, 1978,
1984, 2011 by Biblica, Inc.™ Used by permission of Zondervan. All rights
reserved worldwide. www.zondervan.com The "NIV" and "New International Version" are trademarks registered in the United States Patent and
Trademark Office by Biblica, Inc.™

Italics in Scripture quotations reflect the author's added emphasis

Details, names, and places in some circumstances have been changed to
protect the identities of the persons involved.

Paperback ISBN-13: 978-1-7325025-9-8
ebook ISBN-13: 978-7325025-8-1

www.kristengwilliams.com

Cover design by Scott A. Ryan; Cover photo and back photo of Munni
courtesy of Kristen G. Williams personal archive; Author photo by Anne
Gregoire

Published by New Day Publishing

Printed in the United States of America

For My Precious Munni Bird –
I'll love you for eternity.

PREFACE

Believers often muse that if you want to see God's sense of humor, all you have to do is make plans, then sit back and wait. Nothing could better describe the telling of Kristen G. William's story, *Finding You: A Memoir.*

As Kristen wrote her memoir, she wasn't looking to inspire people with the idea that she spoke to God, or that she heard the voice of God. In truth, reading the story that Kristen tells reminds us that God's voice is divine, and that in our humanity, we are vulnerable to misinterpreting His messages. We are constantly trying to hear God's call, to understand God's voice; and yet, we are limited to our human understanding, bound both by our experiences and desires. So often, we find ourselves *wanting* to hear God say something, and it is precisely our own desires that tend to distort the whispers from our God. Our struggle, then, is to break free of the shackles of our own reality, freeing ourselves to be open to the vulnerability of truly giving ourselves to God.

For Kristen, the shackles of her reality involved her childhood and her understanding of God as an angry and jealous God who doled out punishments for sins. She grew up terrified of a God whom she viewed as judgmental, harsh, and distant. Those were the things that were taught to her about God. Kristen spent years transforming her views of God, accepting Him into her life during high school through Young Life. Kristen learned to love a God who was loving, forgiving, and warm. Those transformative years were important as God called Kristen to Love. He called her to be a mother. He called her to heal the heart of a little girl in India who was haunted by the pain of a childhood that she spent being terrorized. A childhood that left her bloody and bruised. A childhood that left scars painted onto her skin as reminders of her pain and isolation. God used Kristen, then, as a vessel – as a manifestation of His Love – to save Munni. Kristen became a sacrament: a visible sign of God's invisible Love for her daughter. Kristen was Munni's miracle, and Munni was immediately reconnected with Christ through Kristen, as though Jesus, Himself, touched Munni through Kristen. I remember a story that Kristen shared with me as we sat drinking coffee one morning. She told me about how

Munni saw Jesus on the page of a children's book, and Munni looked excitedly into Kristen's eyes, saying, "Jesus." It is profound that a little girl lost in the orphanages of India would recognize Jesus as she met Kristen for the first time.

That moment with Munni came as the result of endless prayer. In Kristen's story, there is a moment she describes – a moment when she gave up herself, crumbled to the floor, and gave herself to God. So often, as Kristen experienced, we are unable to shed sin and the temptations to only allow God to enter our lives on OUR terms. Even as Kristen thought she was giving herself to God, thought that she was obeying His words, Kristen later came to find out that the words she was hearing – though they were God's – were being filtered by her own desires. Only in dying to ourselves, and rising in God's Love and mercy are we able to truly follow Him. Trusting God, then, meant embracing the vulnerability of Kristen losing herself, of losing the picture of her perfect baby, named Sofia. In doing that – in dying to herself – Kristen was able to become the face of Jesus for Munni. There was a connection between Kristen and Munni. A language of Love that escapes the boundaries of human language. A hug. A caress of Munni's skin when Kristen bathed her for the first time. A moment that Kristen rubbed lotion on Munni's skin for the first time, fighting back the tears so that Munni would not be afraid. A moment, a touch, as Kristen soothed her daughter, running her hands across the scars that had been carved into Munni's life. That language, that touch – that Love – is God, made manifest.

Finding God through all of this meant allowing God to breathe His Love into Kristen's life at every moment during the process of adoption. As soon as Kristen tried to interpret God's voice, God's words, they were lost like a whisper in the wind. God's voice often sifts through our lives, wrapping itself around us to comfort us and to guide us, but the moment that we try to grasp that Love, the moment that we try to understand it – to define it in our own terms – we lose it because God's Love, God's Word, is divine. Human language and understanding, then, will always fall short of God's true intention in the same way that writing this book will never truly encapsulate the experiences that Kristen and Munni had. Kristen is able to give us a glimpse of her understanding of God's Truth in the same way that God reveals Himself in little moments in our lives. When we turn to see Him, though, our image is perpetually smeared with the incompleteness of our reality and our perspective. As such, we can never hope to truly and fully understand the messages that God sends us; rather, we are called, as Kristen was, to be vulnerable. To know that we will fall short, but to persist on our path, trusting that God will guide us the way that He led Kristen to Munni.

Kristen's prayer, from the beginning of her writing experience, has been that people's hearts would be changed by reading her story – that people would see the tenderness with which God's Love spills out to his children. She wanted to see how God's Love reaches "the least of these": a little girl rotting away, forgotten, in an orphanage in India. A little girl who had been turned away by many couples looking to adopt. Kristen wanted her readers to see God's grace and mercy as He united Munni, a girl tortured and terrorized in her childhood, with a woman who desperately prayed for a daughter. She wanted her readers to see how God fused their family with His Love. Kristen had found Munni. Kristen had found God in her journey. Munni had found God in Kristen, and Kristen had found God in Munni. This is a story about God's immeasurable Love and about His amazing grace. God's voice spills onto the page in Kristen's writing, allowing God to reveal Himself through Kristen's experiences. We, the readers, drink God's Truth from the pages, perhaps allowing God to seep into our souls if we, too, are willing to be open to sacrificing ourselves. As such, *Finding You: A Memoir* develops a new dimension. The story is not only about Kristen finding herself, finding God, and finding Munni, but also about the reader finding Kristen's story, the reader finding glimpses of himself or herself in relating to the Truths revealed in Kristen's story, and the reader finding God through the experience of reading her story. Thank you, Kristen, for opening your life – and Munni's life – to us.

- S. Joshua Wellen

PROLOGUE
HYDERABAD, INDIA - DECEMBER 2012

I felt the weight of her body against my chest as she drifted off to sleep. Her breathing eased into a peaceful slumber. My arms wrapped around her, I never wanted to let go. The smell of India overwhelmed me as I breathed in earthy campfire filled with aromas of sewage and exhaust. Even with the windows closed, it penetrated our car. I looked out of the dusty window to the bustling city around me, while the ubiquitous sound of car horns filled my ears. The jolting from stop and go gridlock mimicked an amusement park ride. An unspoken rhythm directed the chaotically coordinated traffic. Men who covered their faces with bandanas, zipped in and out of traffic on their motorcycles. The bandanas were an attempt to fight the smog; instead they gave the appearance of outlaws. We drove up next to a huge pair of oxen reluctantly pulling a rickety, wooden wagon; their long, curved horns painted in bright, intricate detail. Three women dressed in sassafras-colored saris danced around the wagon, tossing red flower petals into the air. Elaborate henna decorated their hands and feet. Several men pulled a body, covered in burnt orange and marigold flower petals, from the wagon. As they carefully maneuvered the dead body, the women moved gracefully, encircling the procession. Impervious to the world around them, two men walking with the dancing ladies kept rhythm with dirty, worn drums announcing the rite of passage.

Minal broke the silence in the car, nodding towards the scene on the street, "Kristen, that is a Hindu funeral," she said in her beautiful Indian accent. "They are taking the body to the altar where they will burn it."

The celebration of a life lived. One journey was ending. Our journey was just beginning.

I smiled as I watched the ceremony continue. I hugged Munni closer to me and felt the lump in my throat grow. I never wanted this car ride to end. The love I felt for her was immeasurable.

It took three years of heartbreak to get to this place where I finally held my daughter while she slept on my lap. The last two days were a dream; we spent every minute together. The orphanage allowed me to take custody of her prior to our court hearing, and now, our time together was coming to an abrupt end. I dreaded the next hour, clinging to every detail I could grab. The shape of the scars that riddled her body, the way her short hair curled, the small freckle inside her right ear, the sweet dimple on her cheek, her long fingers, the way her bottom lip pouted when she slept. I gorged my mind with every minute detail I discovered, in hopes that these memories would be the sustenance I needed to get me through the next two months.

We pulled through the massive iron gates and started down the long, bumpy dirt road. Off to the side, yellow dogs laid strewn about like discarded garbage. Dirty papers and piles of cement littered the landscape. Every so often, a green sprout emerged through the rubble. Even in the most unlikely of places, life could not be extinguished. My heart started racing, and I tried to take in deep breaths and slowly exhale. I resisted this moment with every fiber of my being as I hugged Munni tighter and used every ounce of resolve to restrain the sobs that I knew were ready to erupt. The car stopped in front of the entrance. I felt as if all of the air was sucked out of the car. I hugged Munni as tightly as I could. She woke up groggy, and she looked around. Immediately, her face changed at the recognition of the orphanage. She looked at me with questioning eyes, and my heart broke. We got out of the car, walked up to the porch, took off our shoes, and walked inside. I held her tiny hand in mine. I never wanted to let go. I begged Minal to ask someone to please explain to her that I would be coming back for her, that I was not leaving her, and that I had to wait on the court order to be released. Minal spoke Telugu to the director and asked her to relay the message to Munni. I didn't understand what the director said but I prayed that somehow, Munni's precious 6-year-old mind could comprehend what she was being told. Munni looked at the director as she spoke and bobbled her head in typical South Indian fashion. How could she possibly understand? This must all be so confusing to her. I desperately prayed that God would fill her heart with peace and understanding. The director called out, and an ayah came and took Munni back to her room while I filled out more paperwork. It was all a blur as the only thing I could think about was my daughter.

After what seemed like hours, I finished signing all of the papers, and it was time for us to leave. I told Minal I needed to see Munni one last time. We walked down the long hallway, past rooms of sweet, little, Indian faces staring back at us. I focused on the black cement floor as we continued towards her room. It smelled of antiseptic, and I could hardly breathe. Finally, we arrived at her door. I stepped inside to see all of the girls seated on a mat, lined up against the wall. A torn, lopsided curtain that dangled from a flimsy cafe rod, barely covered the bottom of the dirty window. Posters of fruits and vegetables acted as decor. The walls were painted white until about halfway down where they abruptly changed to muddy brown. The paint chipped in striations that almost resembled a pattern. In the corner, two cribs stood side by side with frayed blankets covering tiny, thin mattresses.

The children laughed as I entered the room, and the two ayahs conversed in Telugu. I scanned the faces until I saw her. There she was. Sitting against the wall wearing the white dress I bought her, the pink flower in her hair. Our eyes met and she smiled back at me. Stunning. I walked over and hugged her with all of my might. I heard giggles from the other little girls. I fought back the rage I felt for having to leave her here for two more months. My heart felt torn but I forced myself not to cry because I didn't want to make it worse for her. I whispered in her ear, "I love you Munni. Mommy Munni forever!" I pulled back to look at her beautiful face and her smile grew wider. I melted as I held her face in my hands, and my heart broke when I kissed the scar on her forehead. I told her again how much I loved her. How was I ever going to walk away from her? How could I just leave her here? All I wanted to do was to take her hand in mine and run as fast as I could far, far away from this place.

Minal called to me and told me it was time to leave. I squeezed my eyes shut as I prayed for the strength to leave my daughter behind - an act no mother should ever have to do. I stood up and walked to the door. My heart beat wildly as I turned around to take one last look at my sweet

Munni sitting against the wall. The expression on her face will haunt me until the day I die. Confusion. Betrayal. Sadness. Anger. Her dark eyes pierced my heart.

Minal gently touched my shoulder and guided me out of the room. Tears streamed down my face as we walked down the long hallway and out of the orphanage. My ears ringing, my vision became myopic; the closer we got to the car, the harder it was for me to breathe. I opened the dusty, black door and sat down on the seat. I lost all control and collapsed into a pile of deep, heaving sobs. Minal sat next to me and gently put her hand on my back. No words were spoken.

CHAPTER 1
AUTUMN - 2009

Thirty-nine-years-old and still single, I watched my lifelong dream of motherhood slip through my fingers with each passing day. Another school year had started, marking once again the passage of time and how far away my dream was from becoming a reality. I had wasted so much of my life in dysfunctional relationships and was scared to death that I ruined my chances of ever becoming a mom. The consequences of my actions seemed to mock me as I continued to grow older and the possibilities of motherhood continued to grow smaller.

Ten years prior, while studying Spanish in Mexico, the mother of the family with whom I lived said something that continued to haunt me. I was single and on the verge of turning thirty, which was equivalent to being an old maid in her eyes. One morning, we sat at her kitchen table drinking coffee and eating homemade tortillas hot off of the griddle. She casually asked me if I was waiting for the last bus to leave. I laughed off her question as I dipped my tortilla in the salsa, but it took root in my heart, and it sprouted with worry. Over the years since then, I thought of her words often. It seemed I was late to everything in life; I had yet to reach a milestone in the proper timeframe that society dictated. I was late to graduate from college. I was late to live on my own. I was late to return to graduate school. I was late to start my teaching career. I was late to buy a house. Marriage and a family I could call my own? It appeared those precious gifts would remain permanently on the waiting list.

The thought of never becoming a mom riddled me with trepidation. Marriage was nowhere in sight, so I spent the entire summer praying about whether or not I should adopt. Anxiety chased me, and fear held me captive because even if I could, was it selfish to adopt as a single? Would I be taking a child from the possibility of a two-parent family? Could I provide a loving home for a child? Could I really do it on my own? How would I ever be able to afford it? I grappled with these questions and pleaded to God for clarity. I needed His peace in order to move forward. I wrestled with this decision throughout those long, hot days of summer and hoped He would answer my prayers.

September arrived with clear blue skies. Four weeks into the school year, I noticed the cloud of anxiety dissipating. With each new day, I felt less anxious. During my prayer times, I thought about how, throughout my entire childhood, whenever I was asked what I wanted to be when I grew up, my first response was always a mom. To me, that was the greatest title I could ever hold. In regards to anything else, there was no other yearning the way I desired motherhood. And yet, I struggled to reconcile my truest passion with feelings of guilt that I would bring a child home to a single-parent household. I poured over scripture, trying to find direction. Verse after verse pointed towards caring for the orphan and the widow; over and over they spoke to me, but I never found clarity in regards to my singleness. One day, I had a breakthrough. Reading the book of Matthew, I stumbled upon a verse I had read many times over the years. This time, however, it spoke truth in a way I hadn't previously seen. "When you did it to one of the least of these, you were doing it to me."[1] It was an epiphany as I grasped the truth that God didn't put qualifiers on any of these verses. He didn't say that only couples should care for the orphan. He didn't dictate that only a two-parent family should care for the least of these. He didn't state that only married people should defend the fatherless. No one was exempt from His command to love and care for the vulnerable and to defend their rights. That small nugget of truth slowly sank into my heart. He opened my eyes to the fact that He was the one who had planted the dream of motherhood in me. He was the one who created me to be a mom. And on that warm September afternoon, sitting on my front porch looking out over my flower garden, I heard Him whisper, *"A life with you will be a million times better than a life in an orphanage."*

I caught my breath as I felt that sweet, tingling sensation when I know He is speaking to me. Goosebumps covered my body as I looked up to the clear, blue sky; joy spread through my heart, and excitement quickly followed. For the first time since I had started praying about adopting as a single mom, peace flooded my entire being. I reveled in the euphoria of that moment. I couldn't stop smiling as I finally allowed the realization to sink in that I was going to be a mom!

I soaked in those precious moments and then went inside and started researching international adoption. Up until that moment, I had resisted the strong urge to look into anything adoption-related, for fear I would be disappointed. Now, however, I felt like a kid in a candy shop! There was so much information I couldn't wait to devour. I scrolled through the country list that allowed international adoptions. I clicked on India first. My long fascination with the country made it seem natural. I pulled up an agency's India program page and could hardly contain my giddiness. I started reading about the requirements, the time frames, the children, the cost. In a single moment, all of my joy vanished as quickly as a balloon pops. I couldn't believe what I was reading. I went from pure ecstasy to complete discouragement in a matter of minutes. How could this be right? At least thirty-six months for the process? Singles can only adopt special needs or older children? How does that even make sense? If the child has special needs, wouldn't it be best for the child to be in a home where there is more support? SPECIAL NEEDS? I thought about the classroom down the hall from mine. Many of those kids were nonverbal and some still wore diapers in middle school. Suddenly, my dream of becoming a mom took a twisted turn.

I wanted a baby. A healthy baby.

Discouraged, I leaned back in my chair. I loved India, but nothing about the program lined up with my hopes and desires. Disappointment crept in, hammering its stake in my heart.

I looked at other country program requirements and soon discovered that the adoption world is not friendly towards singles, as only a few countries even allow singles to adopt. This only deepened the stigma I already felt. Great. Just when I thought I was finally going to become a mom, my singleness continued to deny me my dream. I might as well wear a scarlet letter. I knew my chances for a domestic adoption were slim to none and that's why I didn't even allow myself to pursue that as an option. How many single birth mothers would choose another older, single woman to parent their child? The U.S. foster care system is set up for family reunification and adoption through the system is long, complicated, and full of children with medical needs and/or emotional issues. Was it selfish to want a healthy infant? Frustrated, I stood up and called the dogs. I needed to take a walk and process everything. I prayed months for this and now it seemed like I was hitting roadblocks. On top of that, my age continued to haunt me and limit my options even more. With each day, I was getting older and the length of the process gave me anxiety. Three years seemed like an eternity; I felt as if so much time had already been wasted. My heart rate increased as the feelings of fear returned. I put the leashes on my dogs, stepped outside, and took a deep breath. We walked down the steps and began a long walk as the golden autumn sun set behind the giant oak trees that lined my street. Tears stung my eyes, and once again, sadness filled my heart.

CHAPTER 2
WINTER - 2010

Even though discouragement hounded me, I forced myself to fight for my dream. With a renewed sense of purpose, I continued my research for months. I scoured the internet in pursuit of the perfect international adoption program. Relentless in my quest, I sent queries to every agency that had international adoption programs. I clung to that September afternoon when I heard the Lord whisper that a child would be blessed to live with me. I knew adoption was the path I would walk to become a mom, yet something kept gnawing at me. The whole idea of special needs lurked behind me, never in my direct line of vision, but always hanging around like a fog that was slow to disappear. Deep down, a fear inside me wondered if I would ever become a mom to a healthy baby. Residual baggage from my childhood religion caused struggles with my view of God. Unfortunately, a huge part of me still saw him as an angry, revengeful God. I was scared to death I would end up paying for my bad relationship choices by not getting a healthy baby. Terrified that this was how God would even the score, I tried not to think about it.

Late February, after months and months of searching, all of my investigating finally paid off. I stumbled upon a webpage that listed every international adoption program available to U.S. citizens. It was organized by parent requirements and available children. As I scrolled down to the small singles section, I found a country that allowed singles to adopt healthy infants! I couldn't believe my eyes, so I read it several times to make sure I wasn't missing a loophole of any kind. I discovered it was a small program, only allowing each agency to send ten dossiers per year. For this reason, not many people knew about the program.

I called the first agency listed next to this country. Sure enough, it was true: Nepal would allow me to adopt a healthy infant girl! Overjoyed and somewhat in shock, at last I could let myself believe I was going to be a mom! I cried on the phone with the intake counselor. Years of hoping, waiting, and longing for motherhood, and months of searching came pouring out in tears and sobs. I envisioned myself cuddling an adorable, brown-skinned baby who cooed back at me with her big, beautiful, chocolate-colored eyes! The rest of the conversation was a blur. After I heard "yes," all coherent thought left me. Linda emailed me the application, the contract, country guidelines, fees, time table, dossier instructions, suggestions for home study agencies, and a gazillion more documents. My heart raced a million miles a second. Not only was I able to adopt a healthy baby girl, but the projected time line was approximately two months for a referral and six months from referral to bringing her home. I hung up the phone and sat in stunned silence. Finally, the haze cleared, and I could see the path in front of me.

After I completed and submitted the application, I waited over a week for the formal notice of acceptance into the Nepal program. Every time the phone rang, my heart skipped a beat, only to be disappointed. Each day that passed without news felt like an eternity.

Wednesday morning, I woke up and pleaded with God, "Please let today be the day. This would be the best birthday ever if I was accepted today." I felt a mix of emotions as I got ready. I had anxiety over turning 40 and not being where I thought I would be by this age. Even though I was taking steps towards becoming a mom, I struggled with doubt since nothing was official yet; it was a battle to stay positive.

Once I arrived at school, however, my day took on the normal routine of things, and my nerves settled. Then, during third bell, my Spanish students were in the middle of taking a test when I happened to check my personal email. There it was: the subject line read, "Welcome to the Nepal Program!"

I shrieked just a little bit, and a few of my students turned to look at me. "Lo siento." I managed. Thrilled, I tried to contain the pure joy I felt in that moment. "Thank you, Jesus!" I silently prayed as tears filled my eyes. Astounded by His love for me and His faithfulness to answer the prayer I had prayed in the morning, it was the greatest birthday gift I could ever imagine.

Once I got home from school, I raced inside and pulled out the contract.

I had already completed it because what else was I supposed to do while I waited for the approval? I rechecked every single document of the contract. That afternoon, on my 40th birthday, I joyfully signed my name on the dotted line. Happy birthday to me. I drove to the post office and sent the contract via overnight mail. It was official. I couldn't wait to tell my family and friends. Up until this point, I hadn't revealed any of this to anyone because fear had kept me silent. Now, I wanted to shout it from the rooftops!

I dreamed of the moment I would finally hold my baby, and I wondered where she was at that moment. Was she even born yet? I knew that I would name her Sofia Grae. I had treasured the name Sofia in my heart for more than seventeen years, waiting for the day I would be able to give my daughter that beautiful name. Of course, she would have my middle name. I have my dad's middle name, he has his dad's middle name, his dad's dad had his dad's middle name, and so on down the line. I would give her my namesake. I said her name out loud over and over. I called it out in my empty house, imagining her crawling towards me. Simon, my boxer, cocked his head to the side and looked at me like I was crazy. I laughed. I told him, "One day soon, Mister." The image of my daughter materialized in my dreams more and more each day.

I threw myself into discovering everything I could about adopting an infant. I stayed up late researching adoptive breastfeeding, cloth diapers, and making my own baby food. From 'baby wearing' to co-sleeping, I investigated all things associated with attachment parenting. On a trip to buy more envelopes, I found myself wandering aimlessly through the infant section at Target, dreaming of how Sofia would look in all of the adorable baby dresses. A section that once brought me intense sorrow every time I passed it by now flooded my heart with joy and eager anticipation. She consumed my every thought.

Late Friday afternoon, I came home from school and sat on my front porch in the cold, crisp air. I looked out over my garden. It resembled a dead wasteland. Dry, shriveled sticks haphazardly pointed upwards where strong, green stalks once stood. Colorful, fragrant blooms were replaced with thorny, brown canes. A passerby might look upon this mess as a disaster, but I knew the beautiful transformation that was soon to come. And in that moment, I heard Him once again.

"Just as your garden looks dead, so you thought your dream of motherhood. I

FINDING YOU: A MEMOIR

see the beauty that is coming to you."

Tears filled my eyes as I caught my breath in my throat. I quickly prayed, "Can I please have a due date? This journey is so different from what I thought. Could I just have that?"

A few moments of silence kept me holding my breath. I knew it was doubtful He would answer this request. If I had learned anything about God, it's that He doesn't like to reveal too much, too soon. Exhaling, I realized my due date would remain a mystery.

"December 12."

Wait. What? Did I hear Him? I was stunned. He answered me. Oh my goodness, I started counting… NINE MONTHS! I laughed uncontrollably as I couldn't believe it. Never did I expect my adoption timeline to coincide with a pregnancy timeline. Excitement surged through me as I cried happy tears. I thanked Jesus over and over for everything He had done so far. My faith grew by leaps and bounds, and moments like this helped to replace my fear of an angry God with thoughts of a loving God.

* * * * *

Later that night, my sister and brother-in-law came over to take me out to my favorite restaurant for a birthday celebration. I couldn't wait to tell them. They texted me that they were out front waiting. I said goodbye to my dogs, locked the door, and ran down the front steps. I got in the backseat of the car and immediately blurted it out before I even shut the car door. "I have something to tell you." They both turned around to look at me.

"What's up?" Sean asked me.

"Well," I laughed, giddy with excitement, "I'm adopting a baby girl from Nepal!" In my head, fireworks exploded. In reality, Laurie and Sean looked like deer in headlights, both wearing blank stares.

"What?" my sister asked.

I giggled. Full of joy I declared loudly, "I'M ADOPTING A BABY GIRL FROM NEPAL!"

"Wow!" Sean said.

"When?" my sister asked, still stunned from my announcement.

"I signed the papers on my birthday. They said once I complete all of my paperwork, it will take around two months for a referral and then about another six months until I travel to bring her home."

"That's great!" Laurie exclaimed. "What's a referral? How old will she be? When did all of this happen? We didn't even know you were thinking about adopting. Wow. Wow!"

"I know, right? I've been praying about it since last summer but was scared it wouldn't happen. But then, I found the Nepal program and everything started falling into place! Nepal will let me adopt a healthy baby. The other countries that allow singles to adopt won't let you adopt a healthy baby. You have to adopt special needs or an older child."

"That seems so strange that a single parent can only adopt a special needs child. You would think they would want two parents for special needs," my sister pondered.

"That doesn't make sense," Sean added.

"I know. I thought it was weird, too," I agreed. "Nepal was the only country I could find that would allow me to adopt a healthy baby. I knew I would have such a small chance at domestic adoption. I didn't want to wait years for a birth mom to pick me."

"What about a boy?" my sister asked.

"I don't know, it just doesn't feel right. I think because my whole life I've dreamed about having a daughter that I can't even imagine myself with a boy."

"A little girl makes sense," Sean agreed. "You two will be a great team!"

"Thank you. I can't believe it's happening, I am still in shock. So, back to your question, Laurie. A referral is when they present you with a child's file. It will have medical information, whatever social information they have on the child, like how the child came into the orphanage, a picture, and basically any information they have about the child. My caseworker said often times, there is not much information in the files, because the children are abandoned. The matching committee assigns referrals based on your home study, age, and gender requests. I requested a girl, 0-12 months."

"This is awesome, Kristen!" Sean declared. "Her life will be changed forever. I'm excited for you."

"Thank you! I am so excited. You two are the first I've told. I'm going to tell mom and dad at Sunday night dinner and I'm meeting Janet tomorrow to tell her."

"This is great news. Let's go celebrate your birthday and you becoming a mom!" exclaimed Laurie.

I grinned from ear to ear the entire night. My heart overflowed with joy and excitement as I thought about how "40" was going to be the best year of my life.

* * * * *

Saturday morning, I met my best friend for brunch. Janet came into town for my birthday and I couldn't wait to tell her. We met at our favorite breakfast restaurant, a tradition of ours. Ever since she joined the army, she had been relocated out of town. I cherished every moment we got to spend together, and I was thrilled that she came to see me for my birthday. We had just finished ordering our food and were drinking coffee. I couldn't contain myself any longer. "Guess what?" I eagerly asked her.

She looked at me with a sly smile, "What?"

"I'm adopting a baby girl from Nepal!" as a huge smile spread across my face.

Her mouth dropped open. "WHAT?"

"I'm adopting a baby girl from Nepal!" I squealed.

Her eyes started to water as she too, smiled with excitement. "Oh my goodness! I need details! WHEN? You were so meant to be a mom, Kristen!"

"Thank you, Janet! I still can't believe it. You know I've always wanted to be a mom, and honestly, these last few years I've been scared. The closer I got to forty, the more it looked like motherhood was never going to happen for me. My dating record has not been stellar, and I've struggled with so much guilt over my poor relationship choices; almost like losing motherhood was my penance thanks to my stupid, childhood, religious upbringing."

"Whatever. Don't beat yourself up over that. Besides, if anyone was meant to be a mom, it's you. I've thought that for as long as I've known you."

Tears streamed down my face. "Oh my gosh, why do I always cry with you in public?"

She laughed, "That's what we do. We keep things exciting for those around us."

I laughed. "Thanks for being my best friend and always encouraging me.

I love you!"

"I love you too! Just like you always tell me, God can always bring something good out of anything. I can't wait to see you with her in your arms."

"Me either. I constantly try to imagine what she looks like. It's surreal."

"When do you think you will get her?"

"I don't know. But, you want to hear something crazy?"

"Always."

"On Friday, I was sitting on my front porch after school. I prayed and asked God for a due date."

She smiled, "Did he answer?"

I smiled and raised my eyebrows, "Yep."

"No way! When?"

"December 12th"

"Shut up. That's like...9 months away. Just like a pregnancy!"

"I know. I was freaking out. I mean, maybe it was my mind, but I definitely had that tingling sensation I get when I hear from Him. I'm praying and believing it's true!" I exclaimed.

"Awww, I will be praying for that too. What did your parents say?"

"I haven't told them yet. I'm going to tell them tomorrow at family dinner."

"Oh, I bet they are going to be so excited!" Janet mused.

"I hope so. I'm not going to lie, I feel a little nervous telling them. Kind of like I'm sixteen and somewhat asking for their permission. I know it's stupid. It's just that I'm not quite sure how they will respond." I confided in her.

"Well, however they respond, you don't need their permission. You're 40-years-old, stable, and are going to be the best mom! Besides, I think they will be excited for you. I'm sure they have wanted this for you for awhile," she assured me.

"Hmm, I hope so."

"Are you going to tell people tonight?" she asked.

"Nope. I think I want to keep it to my inner circle for a little bit and just revel in it! Besides, I don't want to be crying and trying to sing karaoke!" I laughed.

She laughed, "You're hilarious. But I understand. I didn't run out and tell everyone right away when I found out I was pregnant with Audrey. I just told my family, you, and few other close friends. There is something special about that moment in the very beginning. It's really an intimate time," she reflected, "Ahhh! I am SO EXCITED for you!"

The waitress came and put our food on the table.

"Oh my gosh, these skillets are so delicious. I look forward to this every time I'm home," Janet said.

"Girl. Don't judge me because I'm about to eat this whole thing."

"Oh, me too," she laughed.

* * * * *

Sunday night was our weekly family dinner at my parents' house. I had a video for the Chinese adoption process that my agency included in the welcome packet. Even though I wasn't adopting from China, the video was a beautiful testimony of the incredible gift of adoption. I cried when I watched the families hold their new child for the first time. It was the most beautiful moment. I planned to show the video to my family to break the news. I was happy that my sister and brother-in-law already knew. I wasn't sure how my parents would react. When I thought about telling them, anxiety took over as part of me still felt like a teenager craving her parents' approval. Deep down, I struggled with feeling like a failure because I wasn't married. I never imagined I would be single and childless when I reached forty; instead, I thought I would be dealing with rebellious teenagers, soccer schedules, and school dances. Because this adoption decision was the essence of who I really wanted to be, I was terrified that it wouldn't come to pass. It felt as if I were stepping off an enormous cliff into a free fall. Embarking on the biggest faith journey of my life, I needed to know I had support. I wasn't confident I would find it in my parents. Sharing my desire out loud left me feeling exposed, like I was offering my heart on a silver platter; I hoped it wouldn't be rejected. Part of me wrestled with my own insecurities, and I combined those with fear as I dreaded the possibility of my parents' lack of support.

I decided that I would show them the video after the birthday dinner and before the cake celebration. As I helped my mom clear the plates from the table, my heart started racing and I could feel the adrenaline pulsing through my body. "I have a very special surprise I want to show all of you," I blurted out while picking up the last plate from the table.

"A surprise?" my mom asked.

"Yep. It's a video I want to show all of you," I answered.

My sister and Sean smiled knowingly at me as we all headed into the family room. My dad had his glass of red wine in hand as he sat in his spot on the sofa. My mom sat next to him and looked at me with expectant eyes. My three nephews and my niece gathered around and plopped down in front of the television. I popped in the DVD and pushed play. My heart felt like it was going to jump right out of my chest. Some information about adoption flashed on the screen as the Chinese music continued to play. Next, scenes showed families meeting their precious children for the first time. I could feel my eyes welling with tears as I imagined the moment Sofia would be handed over to me. These images continued for a few minutes and then my oldest nephew Spencer asked, "Wait a minute. Aunt Kristen, are you adopting a baby from China?"

"I am adopting a baby…. but not from China, from Nepal. I signed the papers on my birthday. I'm adopting a baby girl." I choked out with emotional excitement.

"That's great!" Spencer exclaimed as he got up and hugged me.

A.J., Maxwell, and Elizabeth all smiled at me and congratulated me. Max and A.J. hugged me. I couldn't stop smiling as excitement flooded through me.

"So you're not adopting a white baby?" My dad interjected, bringing the happy scene to a screeching halt.

"Richard!" my mom scolded.

I felt my breath catch in my throat. I stood there, stunned. "No, I'm not. I'm adopting a Nepalese baby, so she will be brown," I stammered.

"Hmph. How are you going to pay for it?" he pressed on with his inquisition as he stared at me with a disapproving glare.

"I don't know yet. I have a little bit saved and I'm going to see if I can cash out my 403b," I fumbled.

"That's stupid. Why would you ruin your retirement?" his disdain audible.

"Well, there's not that much in it, but enough to get me started on the adoption. Also, I am still working at Dewey's Pizza serving part time, and I'm going to work as many extra shifts as I can. I don't have it all figured out yet, but I know God has given me the green light on this. I've been praying about it and researching since last summer. I know this is what I'm supposed to do," I responded in my defense. I could feel my face getting hot.

"Well, it's your life. Don't ask me for anything," he concluded as he got up and left the room.

I felt a pit in my stomach as my fears were realized through his reaction. My mom stood up and hugged me. It dawned on me in that moment that not only was I starting the greatest journey of my life, but that I was entering into the biggest battle I would ever experience. The gloves were off, and I knew that I would be fighting with everything I had to bring my daughter home.

*　*　*　*　*

The next Monday at school, I was standing in the copy room waiting for the printer to finish. I tried to dismiss the negativity that my dad had injected into my adoption journey. Instead, I leaned against the mail counter and daydreamed about what Sofia might look like. I was lost in thought as I imagined holding her in my arms… how soft her skin would feel as I kissed her chubby cheeks… her long, black eyelashes… her huge, chocolate eyes staring back at me...

"What's going on? You're GLOWING!"

I jolted back to reality to turn and see my co-worker Christin staring at me with a huge smile on her face.

"Seriously, Kristen, you are glowing! Did something happen?" Christin asked.

I couldn't help but smile and giggle. And then tears of happiness came. "I do have a secret," I told her.

"Spill it!"

"Well," I paused as I looked around to see if anyone else was in earshot, "I'm adopting a baby girl from Nepal!"

"NO! Oh my goodness, that's exciting! When? How old is she? When did this happen? I have so many questions! I'm so excited for you!" she laughed as she hugged me.

"I've been praying about it since last summer, and I finally signed the contract last week on my birthday! I think I am still in shock; it's so exciting, I can't believe it's happening! I just told my family last weekend. I haven't told anyone else yet. It seems surreal. I'm in the beginning stages, so I'm still compiling all of the paperwork. I really hope that I can have my home study completed by May and then my dossier by June."

"WOW! I'm so excited for you! So do you already know who she is?" asked Christin.

"No. I won't be able to be matched with a child until my dossier has been accepted in Nepal. If I can get it completed by June, then my agency will ship it over. They told me that it's possible that I could be matched during the July matching committee. I requested the youngest possible age range, so she will most likely be less than a year old by time I travel to bring her home."

"I'm thrilled for you! You will make a great mom, Kristen." she encouraged me as she hugged me.

"Thank you! I truly feel so blessed, like I'm living a dream. Every morning I wake up, I pinch myself because it still seems so unreal. I have waited and waited and waited to become a mom. Do you know how many weddings and baby showers I've attended? With each one, there was a pain in my heart because I wasn't sure this would ever happen for me. Now that it is, I feel like happiness is spilling out of me."

"Are you going to start telling people?" she asked.

"Little by little, I think. I'm still reveling in the newfound joy!" I answered.

"Ahhhh, I totally get that. I will be praying for you. Please keep me updated. Thanks for starting off my day with such wonderful news!"

I laughed, "Anytime."

CHAPTER 3
SPRING - 2009

The first day of spring break arrived, and I had never been so excited to clean my house. Ever since I scheduled the home study visit, I created a list of everything I wanted to accomplish on my house and in the garden. I bought all of my cleaning supplies, made sure I had great smelling candles, purchased yards of mulch, and planted scarlet red geraniums in the stone pots on my front steps. I made an awesome playlist, banished the dogs to the backyard, and got to work. While dusting the baseboards, I prayed for Sofia. With each stroke of scrubbing the bathroom tile, I thanked God for her and prayed that He would prepare her heart to become my daughter. I prayed for the very first moment we see each other, that when I touched her, she would be flooded with feelings of love, comfort, and peace. I prayed that no fear would encompass her. I asked God to protect our relationship and beseeched Him to shield our bonding as mother and daughter. Energized on a whole new level, with each new task, I became more creative and detailed in my prayers. I begged Him to please let her be as young as possible. I heard about people adopting older children and I couldn't understand it. Hadn't they heard of Reactive Attachment Disorder? Why would someone willingly put themselves in that situation? Since I was going to be a first time mom, I justified desiring a baby. Surely, God would honor my prayers.

I attacked the home study and the dossier simultaneously since many of the required documents overlapped one another. I created two checklists for each, and meticulously updated them with a swift check each time I obtained a required credential. Surprised at how much I accomplished during my break, I almost finished all of the paperwork. In addition, my house received the most thorough cleaning it probably ever had in its 80 years of existence. I completed twelve hours of Hague training in order to fulfill the requirements for international adoption. I learned about attachment and bonding, behavior and mental disorders, culture and identity, effects of institutionalization, effects of stress, fetal alcohol syndrome, malnutrition, older child adoption, the effects of trauma, prenatal exposures, sensory integration disorder, and how to live as a conspicuous family. It was an overwhelming amount of information to process, but I enjoyed the intellectual stimulation, and I felt more prepared than ever.

Finally, I called about my 403b and secured the withdrawal of my account. I didn't even care that a penalty was involved; Sofia was worth it! Combined with the money I had saved from my part-time serving job, I had enough to pay for the first set of agency fees and part of the prepayment of a referral fee. I was ecstatic! Everything was falling perfectly into place and each night I laid my head on my pillow, I fell asleep dreaming about Sofia.

At last, the day of the home study visit arrived. The night before, I tossed and turned due to the bundle of nerves in my stomach. Simon was not pleased with my restlessness. It felt strange to have my whole life under a magnifying glass; every tiny fiber of my existence was inspected to ensure my capabilities of motherhood were intact.

After school, I raced home, and the first thing I did was light the candles. I read somewhere that a home filled with the aroma of baked goods sends positive subliminal feelings to guests; I pulled out all the stops and chose the scent "warm baked apple pie." I smiled, thinking I was hitting it out of the park because what smells better than that? I sequestered the dogs to the basement and sat down to view all of my hard work. The house looked immaculate. I grinned, feeling accomplished. Wait, is it too clean? I stood up and walked around. Maybe everything was too perfect. Would she think I wouldn't allow for creativity, crafts, and games? I walked to the mantle and moved one of the picture frames out of place. I turned it just a little bit, enough to disrupt the rigid, straight line. I sat back down and surveyed my surroundings again. How do I find the balance of looking clean, but also that someone lives here? I stood up and walked to the sofa. I picked up the throw, wrapped it around me, and then dropped it back on the top cushions. I made some quick adjustments. That looked better. Less perfect and more comfy. I sat down again and looked at my watch; ten more minutes until her arrival. It seemed like an eternity.

At last, the doorbell rang and the dogs howled in the basement. My pulse quickened as I walked to the door and opened it.

"Hello!" I tried to sound cheery and relaxed, but I felt quite certain she could see my heart beating in my chest.

"Hi. I'm Brenda. It's nice to finally meet you in person!" she said as she extended her hand to shake mine. "You have a lovely garden."

"Thank you! It's a creative outlet for me."

"I can see that!"

"Please come in! I put my dogs in the basement in case you aren't a dog person," I explained.

"Oh, I love dogs, so whatever makes you comfortable," she answered. "Besides, I will see them when I do the safety inspection."

"Okay. Well, as I tell everyone, if you blink you will miss the tour! This is small house living at its finest," I joked nervously.

"That's fine. What year was your house built?" she inquired.

"1930. There are several on this street that are the Sears Roebuck Catalog Houses."

"Oh! That's interesting," she replied.

"We can sit at the table if that's alright? Would you like a drink?" I asked as we moved towards the dining room table to sit down.

"Oh, I'm fine," she replied as she sat down at the table. "Okay, Kristen, let's get started," she said as she pulled out an enormous binder and legal notepad. She clicked her pen and wrote my name at the top of the paper. Without looking up from the notepad, she asked, "What is your motivation to adopt?"

Out of the gate with the zinger. Wow. I guess I thought there would be more small talk or basic questions before the headliner. I could feel my pulse quicken as I flashed back to all the cop sitcoms I watched in my childhood. I could visualize the criminal in the interrogation room; the bright light shining down, and beads of sweat forming on his forehead. I shifted in my chair, nervous my response would fall short of her approval. It was intimidating to know that this woman held the power in her pen of whether or not my dream of motherhood would come to fruition. Even though rationally, I knew I had nothing to fear, the depths of this inquisition into every facet of my life was a pressure unlike anything I had ever experienced. She kept a perfect poker face as I explained my journey up to this point. With every probing question she posed, and my thoughtful answer to each, not a hint of expression could be found in her countenance. It was unnerving. How did my parents discipline me when I was young? How would I discipline? Would I use corporal punishment? Had I ever been sexually abused? Was I ever convicted of a crime? Do I drink alcohol? How would I incorporate her culture into our daily lives? Do I have friends of color? How will I handle being a conspicuous family? What is my net worth? What special needs am I open to? Do I have a support system in place? Is my family supportive of my adoption plans? What will I do for a father figure for my child? After almost two hours of cross-examination, I tried my hardest to remain composed. The tears finally fell when I tried to articulate that becoming a mother was what I wanted most in life.

"I'm sorry," I squeaked out, "It's just that there's nothing I want more than to be a mom. I never imagined I would be forty, single, and childless. Life didn't go how I dreamed it would, and now that I'm at this place, where the possibility of finally becoming a mom is in front of me. It's emotional." I wiped away my tears and tried to steady my voice. "I think because it's taken so long to get to this point, I value the importance and significance of being a mom more than I ever could have if I had become a mom ten or fifteen years ago. If motherhood had happened the natural way, I don't think I would have understood the honor of what it means to be responsible for shaping another human being and raising that person in love. Going through all of this paperwork, all of the doctor appointments, acquiring all of the documents, completing all of the coursework, the references, the background checks: All of it has impressed upon me the weight of this responsibility. I couldn't be more excited and eager to finally be at the point of realizing this lifelong dream."

For the first time, Brenda looked up from her legal notepad where she had been meticulously documenting my every response. "Kristen, I think you will make a wonderful mother."

My throat tightened and tears filled my eyes once again. "Thank you," I managed to say in a high-pitched voice. "That means so much." I continued to wipe my tears.

"Well, it should take me about two weeks to compile all of the information into the report format. I will email you a draft to proofread and make any edits you see fit. After that, I will send it to your agency for them to approve. Once they approve it, I will send you three original, notarized copies. Does that sound okay for you?" she asked.

"You have no idea. I am thrilled. Thank you so much, Brenda!"

After her safety inspection of my house, she collected her things and we made our way to the front door. After I walked her out, I felt completely weightless and simultaneously filled with joy and eager expectation.

"Your garden is truly a delight. I love all of your flowers, especially the roses," she remarked.

"This garden is such a blessing to me," I answered, "I've learned so much about myself through tending to all of the flowers, watching it evolve, and continually planning for new ideas. I can't imagine not having it."

"Well, you can see that it is cared for with love. I imagine your daughter will enjoy it as well. Look for my email in about two weeks."

"Thank you so much, Brenda. And believe me, I will be stalking my email!"

"I don't doubt it," she laughed as she got into her car. I watched as she drove away. I turned towards the house and jumped up and down with excitement. The home study was a success, and I was one step closer to Sofia.

I picked up my phone and called my agency. I wanted my caseworker to know that the home study went well.

"Hi, Linda. This is Kristen."

"Hi Kristen. I was just looking at your file. How is your process coming along?"

"That's why I'm calling you. I just had my home study visit and it went great! She said that she will have the report completed in about two weeks and that she will send both of us three notarized copies."

"Perfect! You are moving in record time! Now you will want to shift your focus to the immigration side of things. In order for you to be considered for the 2010 matching committee, we need to have your dossier in Nepal no later than July 10th. The cutoff for our agency's ten dossier submission for 2010 is July 15th. If your dossier is not completed and in country by that time, I'm sorry to say that you will then be placed on the waiting list for the 2011 matching committee next April. I explained this to you in our original phone conversation. The immigration piece usually takes between 4-6 weeks, so it looks like you are definitely on track to have everything submitted for 2010. Our goal is to ship the ten dossiers by June 23rd. We want to ensure ample time for shipping and receiving. You will also need to compile your dossier and send that to us. The immigration approval will come to us directly, so we would like to have your dossier here, ready to go, upon receiving notification of your immigration approval."

"Oh my goodness, Linda. My heart is beating so fast!" I replied.

"That's expected," she laughed. "You can fill out the I-600a form. This form gives you permission from the Department of State to adopt an orphan from another country. The instructions and the template were included in your welcome email. However, you cannot submit it until you have your home study in hand, since that is a required document. While you are waiting for her to compile the report, fill out the I-600a and assemble all of the other required forms. That way, once you receive the home study, you can mail the immigration packet immediately. As I said before, it can take up to 4-6 weeks. It all depends upon which officer you are assigned and how quickly they decide to process. You don't want to have a hand in slowing anything down."

"I have everything for the dossier except the home study and immigration. Tonight, I will double check that everything is in order. Believe me, I won't do anything to slow this process down." I assured her.

"I don't doubt you for one minute." she replied. "I've been amazed at your efficiency and speed. Let's talk again once you or I receive the home study. Now, go out and celebrate this milestone!"

"I will. Thanks again, Linda. Have a great day!" I smiled as I hung up the phone.

* * * * *

Two weeks later, I found my home study waiting for me in the mailbox when I got home from work. I shifted into overdrive and started compiling my dossier. I had been keeping every document I obtained filed in a binder, ready for this moment. I double checked that I had every single required credential. Giddy with excitement, I couldn't believe I was about to send my dossier to my agency. I took out my checkbook and wrote a check for the last fee. I was still in disbelief that I was able to cash out my 403b; combined with the money I was making from serving part-time, it paid for everything up to this point. I knew I still needed at least fifteen thousand dollars for travel, orphanage donation fee, and final immigration visa fees, but I wasn't going to let that future worry dampen my spirits. Today was a celebration of reaching a major milestone in my adoption journey. I put everything together, paper clipped my check on top of the stack of papers, and drove to the FedEx office as fast as I legally could.

I walked in and put my mountain of paperwork on the counter. I stared at it. My whole life was in those papers. A young woman came over to help me.

"Do you want to ship those in a box or an envelope?" she inquired.

"I want the safest option, so I'm thinking a box. That's my whole life right there." I replied.

"You're whole life in a box it is," she declared. "That must be pretty important."

"Actually, it's the best thing I've ever done - I'm adopting a baby girl from Nepal." I gushed.

"Wow! That's amazing and crazy. You know why it's crazy?" she asked me.

"No, why?"

"Because just last week, there was a lady who came in here with her little baby boy that she just brought home from Ethiopia. He was the cutest thing. OH! I know what - when you get your baby girl home, you should adopt a baby boy from Ethiopia." she proclaimed.

My skin started tingling and my whole body felt warm. My mind started racing. What did she just say? God, is that you speaking to me through her?

"I could just see you with two brown babies. I bet I'll see you back here for your second!" she continued in confidence.

I just stood there and smiled at her with a dumb expression on my face. Two? I thanked her, took my receipt, and walked out the door. My thoughts were all over the place. I got in my car and immediately started praying. "Do you want me to adopt two children God? Was that you speaking to me?" I only get that feeling when God is telling me something to which I'm supposed to pay attention. Around and around in my mind, visions were swirling.

My phone snapped me back to reality. I answered, "Hey, Wiggins!"

"Williams! How is everything going?" my good friend Kristen asked. We met in 1995 as Young Life summer staffers and instantly became kindred spirits. Since our first names were exactly the same, we always called each other by our last names. Even though she was married now, her maiden name still stuck.

"I just sent my dossier to my agency - I can't believe it!"

"No way! That's incredible. Oh my goodness Williams, I just thought about what you told me the last time we talked and realized that you are so on track for your due date! Do you think it could still happen in December?" Wiggins asked.

"I do! My agency said as long as I can get my immigration approval before the June 23 deadline to ship the dossiers, I will be in the 2010 batch. Linda thinks that I will receive a referral quickly," I reported.

"Ahhhh I am so happy for you! I will continue to pray. Keep me posted."

"I will," I promised.

"Love you, friend!"

"Love you, too!"

I hung up the phone and smiled. I sat in my car and allowed myself to feel all of the happiness in that moment.

CHAPTER 4
A DOOR CLOSES - AUGUST 6TH, 2010

"Kristen, are you still there?" I could hear Linda's voice through my phone. I felt like I was underwater, and her words were jumbled. My heart raced as my palms sweated profusely; I seemed to be breathing through a straw and I gasped for each breath.

"Yeah," I managed to squeak out between sobs. "How is this happening? What does this mean? I'm not bringing home my baby, am I?"

"We've been in contact with the Department of State ever since they released the statement on the suspension of adoptions from Nepal. We are working hard to understand their expectations and what this will look like for the future of the Nepal adoption program. We are asking our families to sit tight and know that we are doing everything in our power to figure out the best solution and next steps," Linda stated in an attempt to quell my fears.

It didn't work. I couldn't even focus on what she was telling me. All I heard was the U.S. Department of State shut down adoptions from Nepal. In my heart, I feared Sofia wasn't coming home. Linda rattled on about regulations, investigations, and who knows what else. The only thought in my head was, *"I just lost my baby."* My beautiful baby that I never even met. My sweet Sofia who didn't even have a face. My daughter for whom I'd been waiting years. I didn't have a referral when the DOS announced earlier today they were suspending all adoptions, so there was no way I would be getting a referral now. I felt like I was going to vomit.

What is going on? My mind raced back to the online Nepal adoption group this morning when the announcement was released. Everyone was frantic. People were throwing around the words "closed," "stuck," "Hague transition." I didn't even know what the Hague Convention was; I only knew that my training was Hague. It was a frenzy; everyone stating their opinions, comparisons to the Vietnam program, suggestions of switching countries. People were jumping ship as fast as they could. All of it made me nauseous, and I couldn't process any of it. I sat there stunned.

"I will contact you with every new piece of information we receive. It may be a phone call, but most likely it will be email," Linda jolted me back to the present. "I know this sounds trite Kristen, but try to keep a positive attitude."

"Okay," I mumbled before I hung up the phone. I felt like I was being suffocated. I got up and put on my running shoes. I had to get out of my house and into fresh air. I bolted out the door and started running. How could this be happening? *What are you doing, God? I don't understand!* I thought back to the beginning of summer and how he had orchestrated everything so perfectly. My fingerprint appointment for immigration was miraculously rescheduled for 3 weeks earlier. Had that not happened, my immigration approval wouldn't have come in time for my dossier to be shipped to Nepal by the July deadline. The deadline that determined whether I would be registered with the matching committee in Nepal or if my dossier would be put on the waiting list to be submitted with the April 2011 batch. Getting my dossier to Nepal by July determined that I was the last of the 2010 dossiers. If God didn't want me to get Sofia, why would he have allowed everything to fall so perfectly into place, at just the right times? What about my December due date? Was this some kind of sick joke?

I kept running. Tears streamed down my face as doubt flooded my heart. Was God punishing me for poor decisions I made in the past by withholding the only thing I have ever wanted in life? I fought hard against the internal whispers that screamed I was getting what I deserved. The angry and revengeful God of my childhood religion loomed over me. It crushed my spirit.

CHAPTER 5
UNEXPECTED HOPE - SEPTEMBER, 2010

"Hello. Am I speaking with Kristen?"

"This is she," I replied.

"Hi Kristen. This is Susan, the director at One World. I wanted to personally welcome you to the Congo program; we are excited for you to build your family through adoption!"

"Oh, Susan, you have no idea how happy this makes me! I don't know if Terri told you my story but I got caught in the Nepal suspension, and I've been heartbroken. This is the first time I've felt hope that I will actually become a mom."

"Yes, she did. I'm so sorry about Nepal, Kristen. That's a difficult situation. The good news is that the Congo program is moving quickly and depending on how soon you can get your home study converted, you could be home with your baby this summer!"

"I don't think I can even wrap my mind around this! I've had so many conversations with Terri about doing a concurrent adoption, what that looks like, how it would play out, and she told me the same thing. She said my baby boy would be home from the DRC before my daughter would be home from Nepal. I've been following several of the pipeline families who have been stuck in Nepal, and none of them are home yet."

"It is very sad that this is happening. But we have to trust that the proper procedures will take place, and all the children will be cleared to go home to their families. You are not the only Nepal family we have who is signing up for a concurrent adoption with the Congo. There is a tremendous need for families for the orphans in the Congo. That country has been ravaged by war and disease, and the children are the innocent victims in all of it. You will be making a tremendous difference - and I am talking life and death difference - in the life of your child," Susan informed me.

"Wow. I don't think I've grasped how dire the situation is. My heart is filled with hope to be on this journey. Thank you for welcoming me into the program. Terri has been incredible and so patient in dealing with my incessant questions, concerns, doubts, and just plain craziness. I'm excited to work with her as my family counselor!"

"Terri is wonderful. Her experience as an adoptive mom is incredibly helpful and she understands the emotional aspect so well. We are blessed to have her on our staff!"

"Thanks again for this phone call. You made my day!" I hung up the phone and exhaled. What a journey this was becoming. I thought back to that day in the FedEx office when I sent my dossier to Nepal.

The words of FedEx worker still rung in my ears, "I know, when you get your daughter home, you should adopt a baby from Ethiopia."

It wasn't Ethiopia, but here I was, starting my second adoption. It felt like a whirlwind with no logical reason, yet so many answered prayers and pieces fell perfectly into place. Still shellshocked from the Nepal suspension, I wasn't even looking at other country programs or contemplating another adoption for that matter. I was stunned when Terri emailed me two weeks after the DOS announcement. Her agency was one that I had emailed in my initial inquiry for Nepal - eight months ago. It seemed odd that she contacted me out of the blue. Once I shared my Nepal situation with her, she suggested I do a concurrent adoption. I had no idea what that was or how it worked. We emailed and talked for weeks before I felt certain that this was an avenue I was supposed to pursue. I quickly realized that I will never understand God's ways or His plan. It was scary to step out in faith and pursue this adoption, but peace was the predominant feeling that filled my being.

CHAPTER 6
THE MOST SORROWFUL TIME OF THE YEAR
- DECEMBER, 2010

As December 12th approached, the pit in my stomach grew. I felt stupid for believing that I heard God about a due date. Feelings of unworthiness crowded my thoughts. Who was I to think the God of the universe would whisper a due date to me? Things with the Congo adoption were progressing, but nothing could satiate the longing for my daughter. I constantly wondered if I would ever bring Sofia home.

December is supposed to be the most magical month of the year, filled with love, wonder, friends, and family. All I felt was bitterness and despair. Nine months ago, I was certain I would be celebrating my first Christmas with Sofia. My visions of her sitting on the floor, babbling away while I trimmed the tree, were shattered like a broken ornament. With each passing day, all of the memories I had created in my mind vanished as my dream dangled further and further in front of me. She was slipping away, and sorrow filled my heart.

Eighty pipeline families were stuck in the Nepal suspension. Five of those families received visas for their children, and three of them made it home. It had been four months since the DOS issued the suspension, and only three families were home with their children. Three families. Seventy-eight were still waiting. Many of them flew to Nepal at the announcement of the suspension, only to be left stranded by the hands of government bureaucracy. The reality of the situation and the lack of urgency in how it was being resolved left me feeling a permanent punch to the gut.

Desperation and hopelessness greeted me with each new day. December 12 loomed over me like an ominous cloud. I dreaded its arrival with every fiber of my being. Finally, early Sunday morning, I woke to the day I had been dreading. It was here. And she was not. My boxer hogged half of my bed instead of my daughter. I felt utterly lost. My insides hurt in ways I'd never experienced. Anger, heartbreak, despair, embarrassment for believing, confusion, and grief all formed a giant ball in my gut, knotted together in an intricate mess. Paralyzed by emotion, I laid in my bed staring at the ceiling.

"DING!"

The sound of a text startled me. I looked at my phone. It was a text from Wiggins.

"Praying extra prayers for you today, friend. Love you."

Tears streamed down my face as I rolled over and sobbed into my pillow. How was this real? I drifted off into a grief-stricken slumber.

*　*　*　*　*

Caught in a downward spiral, I knew I was in trouble, so I forced myself to partake in Christmas traditions in the hopes it would snap me out of the depression that enveloped me. I begrudgingly listened to the Christmas channel on the radio while driving my car. I sat through *It's A Wonderful Life* and didn't even cry; a red flag waved in my brain. I worked as many shifts at the restaurant as I could, anything to keep me from being alone with my thoughts. My heart physically hurt, and I couldn't see a way out of the pain.

The last three weeks were filled with prayers, tears, and begging God for relief, a sign, or anything to show that He even remotely cared about me. All of my pleas were met with silence. Although I had zero desire to do it, I decided to buy a Christmas tree. I needed something to help me escape this emotional prison that held me captive. It was four days before Christmas, and I doubted myself for even trying to appear festive. Scrolling through my holiday music, I chose Handel's *Messiah* to entertain me while I half-heartedly trimmed the tree.

In the middle of wrapping the third string of lights, my heart fluttered as the lyrics broke through what I had tried to tune out:

"Every valley, every valley
shall be exalted
shall be exalted

and every mountain and hill made low,
the crooked straight, and the rough places plain,
the crooked straight, the crooked straight, and the rough places plain."[2]

Those words pierced my heart, and I cried. What a crooked path I had traveled so far. Never in my wildest dreams could I have imagined the twists and turns this journey would take. I was exhausted and spent, and in desperate need of encouragement. Those sweet lyrics breathed life into my spirit so that I felt the tenderness of God. It was as if He whispered those lyrics to me, gently informing me of His power; He would make my path straight. I didn't know how, but I knew He would. The mountains and hills that stood in my way, He would tear down. He would lead me to Sofia, wherever she may be.

CHAPTER 7
THE LEVEE BROKE - MAY 2011

"Excuse me! Coming through!" I warned the crowd while holding two large pizza trays above my head as I navigated through the sea of people waiting for a table. We were slammed. It seemed like everyone in the city wanted to eat at Dewey's on this rainy night. The Friday rush started almost immediately after I clocked in; something about rain makes people dine out. I was thrilled because I knew I would make great tips, they would make a welcome addition to my Congo adoption fund. I saved everything I made from my second job waiting tables, and the growth I saw in my savings account encouraged me; however, I still fell significantly short on the funds needed to complete the adoption. Last month, I applied for a grant through Help Us Adopt, an organization that actually awarded grants to singles. I wouldn't find out until June if they picked me or not. In what seemed like a sea of adoption granting organizations, only three did not discriminate based on marital status. The single stigma followed me into every realm of the adoption world, taunting me like a playground bully and adding to the stress of this unpredictable journey.

"Any news on the adoptions?" asked Beth, one of my Friday night regulars.

"I wish," I responded, "I'm still waiting for a referral from the Congo. I've been stuck at number seventeen on the waiting list. And I've heard nothing on the Nepal front."

"Hang in there, things are bound to change. I can't believe it's been this long already. At least you are moving up on the waiting list for the Congo." she tried to encourage me.

"That's what I keep telling myself so that I don't end up in a straight jacket." I jokingly replied.

"That wouldn't be good. Who would bring me my Oberon?" her husband Mark chimed in.

"Right?" I answered, "So, are we going with the usual? X-Pepperoni and a side peppercorn ranch salad, tomatoes on the side, with extra ranch dressing?"

"You got it!"

I gathered their menus and walked back to the server stand. A heaviness started to descend upon me and all of the sudden, I didn't want to talk to anyone anymore.

I could feel myself shutting down as I circled the restaurant refilling drinks, clearing dirty dishes, mindlessly taking orders. I ghost-walked through the rest of the shift as my thoughts haunted me. When my regulars asked about my adoption process, a switch went off and reality smacked me across the face, waking me from the denial I had been living in for the last month. In April, I saw it on the Department of State's webpage. Nepal issued an official statement on the adoption process. Nepal stated that they would not allow adoptions to the United States to take place under any circumstances; whether the child was abandoned or surrendered, adoption would not be an option. This was the first time I had seen anything issued from Nepal. Up until that notice, everything had come from the United States. It was clear that the suspension from the United States government offended Nepal, and they retaliated with their own statement. It took a month for the realness of the consequences of that notice to sink into my mind; and it happened during the busiest shift of the week.

Standing in the middle of the restaurant while sweeping my section, the blinders fell from my eyes. Despite my desperate pleas to God throughout the evening, begging for it to be wrong, He tenderly exposed the truth that I had tried to hide but knew deep within my heart. Sofia was not coming home from Nepal.

I somehow managed to finish my shift and complete all of my side work. I walked up to the bar to do my cash out with the new manager; this was his first solo Friday night shift. I laid the credit receipts, my server report, and my money on the bar and started to do the calculations for tip outs and cash owed to the restaurant.

"Why do you look so sad?" Andy innocently asked me.

My face crumpled. I no longer had the strength to hide my grief. I slid off of the barstool and ran to the bathroom. I locked the door, slumped down onto the floor, and lost control. Like a shattered wine glass, sorrow and despair poured out of me, staining everything. Every time I thought I could get up, new waves of heaving sobs took over me. Nine months of bottled up emotions finally exploded while I sat on the bathroom floor. I stared at the broken shards of my dream of Sofia, scattered into a million little pieces. I couldn't see how it would ever be made whole again.

After about ten minutes, I got up and looked at myself in the mirror. A red face soaked with tears stared back at me. Mascara ran down my cheeks like tattoos, permanently marking the heartbreak I felt.

"Get your shit together!" I yelled in my head as I looked at the mirror, hoping to startle myself back to a place of control.

Deep breaths. Deep breaths.

I splashed cold water on my face and blotted it with paper towels. No matter how hard I willed myself to stop crying, the tears still fell.

Finally, I grabbed another wet paper towel, opened the door, and walked back to the bar. Tears ran down my face. Mischa cleaned the bar while Andy stapled the paperwork.

"What's wro—?" Andy started to ask, but Mischa elbowed him in the ribs. She looked at me with compassion and I appreciated her silence.

"I can't do my cash out," I managed through tight vocal chords, "I need to leave," as the tears fell faster.

"Don't worry about it. I'll do it and put your tips in an envelope for you and you can get it whenever," Andy replied. "I hope you're okay."

I could feel the sobs coming again so I quickly turned and walked through the kitchen out the back door. I could barely see through the tears by time I reached my car. I got in, laid my head on the steering wheel, and released the outpouring of emotion that flooded my heart. Wails of grief erupted from deep within my soul.

I lost her. I lost my daughter.

CHAPTER 8
RELEASE - JUNE 6TH, 2011

"I feel guilty and I don't even understand why I feel this way," I confessed to Linda, my caseworker for the Nepal adoption.

"I think what you are feeling is very natural. You've been connected to Nepal for over a year and thought that you would be going there to meet your daughter. But, I've seen this time and time again in the twenty years I've been working in adoption. Whether a birth mother changes her mind at the last minute, or a family doesn't accept the first referral, or a referral falls through, when they finally get the child they bring home, they always say, 'THIS child is our child and perfect for our family.' Through the twists and turns, the families find their way to their child. Kristen, your daughter is not in Nepal."

My heart ached, and tears stung my eyes as I listened to her blunt reply. "I know that deep down in my heart, but I guess withdrawing from the program feels scary because that makes it one hundred percent real."

"I understand your hesitations because it does make it final; however, I do believe that it will be a very long time before Nepal gets the systems in place that will satisfy the U.S. government to the point they will lift the suspension."

"Ugh. I know what I'm supposed to do… I just don't have the courage to do it," I replied.

"There is no rush. Take your time. Grieve your loss. When you feel ready and confident, let me know, and I will try to help you continue your path towards motherhood. If there is anything I can do to help you in the meantime, please don't hesitate to call me."

"Thank you, Linda. I really appreciate it. I'm going to spend some more time praying and hopefully will finally get some peace about it." I hung up the phone and felt gross. The last two weeks were a fog of sadness. I trusted God through this entire process, and He provided and showed up in ways that I couldn't have imagined. But this last blow left me battling my mind as I felt stuck in a situation that seemed incredibly cruel and awful. I forced myself to trust that He had a better plan. He had to. And I had to trust that somehow, someway, Sofia would make it home, but the question from where had been plaguing me. About three weeks before my epic meltdown at the restaurant, the special needs program in India starting making appearances in my emails from several of the agencies I had originally contacted when I was researching Nepal. I thought it was weird. Their notices of how this program had children immediately available for adoption planted a seed of panic in my heart. I feared that God was leading me to a special needs child from India. The gnawing feeling I had from the beginning about special needs never left; it remained silently waiting in my peripheral vision. But the more I felt His nudge towards special needs, the harder I pushed it away. I was not in a position to adopt a special needs child, nor did I want to. I wanted my healthy baby girl.

Two hours passed since I talked to Linda. I worked in my garden to clear my mind, but the special needs program kept popping up in my thoughts. How could this be? Why would God do this to me? Does He really want me to surrender my dream of a healthy baby? Is that the payback I get?

My ringtone rattled me from my negative stream of consciousness. "Hello?"

"Hi. Am I speaking with Kristen Williams?"

"Yes," I replied hesitantly.

"Hi Kristen! This is Becky Fawcett from Help Us Adopt."

I caught my breath. "Hi Becky!" I tried to sound cheery and relaxed, but already my palms were sweaty.

"This is one of the absolute favorite parts of my job because I get to tell you that you are our 50th family to receive a grant from Help Us Adopt! Congratulations!"

I started to cry. "Oh my goodness, Becky! You have no idea how incredible it is to get this phone call from you on this day. I can't believe it!"

"Well, you better believe it. We hope this helps in getting your baby boy home from the Congo! Do you have a referral yet?"

"No, I don't. I've been stuck at number seventeen on the waiting list," I managed to reply before my voice cracked. I shouldn't have said the word stuck. I couldn't hold it back, and sobs took over. My entire dream of motherhood was stuck. Nothing seemed to move forward, and I couldn't take it anymore. Through broken sentences filled with sorrow, I poured out my heart to Becky and told her all about Nepal and the heartbreak I experienced. She listened with compassion and empathy as I blubbered on, and then she spoke words that stopped me cold.

"Kristen, your daughter is not in Nepal."

"What?"

"Your daughter is not in Nepal," Becky revealed to me with such assurance in her voice. "I don't know where she is, but she is not in Nepal. And I do know one thing, you will find her."

"I can't believe you just said that. I spoke with my Nepal family coordinator earlier today and she told me the same thing, worded exactly how you just said it to me." I sat there stunned as I felt the tingling sensation that started in my fingers, continued up my arms, flowed through my body, down my legs, all the way to my feet. "Becky, the last few weeks I've had this nudging in my heart that I'm supposed to adopt a special needs child from India. This can't be a coincidence that both of you said the identical sentence to me that she is not in Nepal. This is going to sound crappy, I know, but I'm scared of special needs. And I'm scared to death that my daughter will end up being a special needs child."

"I don't know the path you are supposed to take, but I will tell you this: Don't let your fear stop you. When you find her, you will know that she is the one; whether she is special needs or not. You will know that she is your daughter."

We talked for a few minutes more and then ended the conversation. I sat on my porch and looked at my garden. What in the world was happening? I could not wrap my mind around it.

I picked up the phone and called my mom.

"Hi, Sweetie! What are you doing?" Just the sound of her voice brought tears to my eyes.

"Hi, Mom. Guess what?"

"I don't know," she answered.

"I just got a phone call that they awarded me the grant from Help Us Adopt," I managed to say in a normal voice.

"That's WONDERFUL, Kristen! When will you get-"

"Mom," I interrupted her, "I think I'm supposed to adopt a special needs child from India." As soon as I finished stating my revelation, a wave of peace washed over me. It was a strange sensation.

"Oh," my mom replied, trying to sound supportive. I could hear her uncertainty.

The words came tumbling out as I rehashed everything to her. As I listened to my own words explaining what had transpired over the last few weeks, my confidence in special needs adoption grew, and I felt the fear evaporating. All of the sudden, my feelings of being stuck disappeared. My mom and I talked for a little while longer, and then I couldn't take it anymore. "Mom, I have to go. I have to make one more phone call. I'm going to officially withdraw from the Nepal program." I felt as if ten thousand pounds fell off of my back.

"Are you sure?" my mom asked.

"One hundred percent," I replied.

CHAPTER 9
THE FIRST TIME I SAW HER FACE
- JUNE 16TH, 2011

I stared at the sea of faces as I scrolled down through the waiting list of hundreds of children. There were so many of them that they all seemed to blend together. I felt sick to my stomach and completely heartbroken. It overwhelmed me to think that each one of them had a story of how they ended up in an orphanage. They all had special needs. Some of those needs scared me to death. Some of them seemed manageable. All of them were tragic.

I spent the last week calling agencies and interrogating them about their India program. One agency, in particular, was extremely helpful. The family counselor patiently answered all of my questions and filled in the gaps with information I didn't even know to ask. He gave me a general outline of what I needed to do to get my dossier switched to India. He also spoke to me about a little 3-year-old girl who had mild cerebral palsy. He had been advocating for her and thought she would be a good match for me. Even though I surrendered my idea of a healthy baby, and now felt confident in pursuing a special needs child, I still wrestled with the age part of this adoption. I struggled to let go of my dream of adopting an infant, and three seemed so old compared to a baby. I thought about all of the milestones I would miss adopting someone her age, and it made me sad. I told him I needed some time to pray and think about it.

In the meantime, I found another agency who had a photo listing of all of the waiting children in their international adoption program. Some of them were from China, some were from South Korea, others were from Russia and Eastern Europe, and of course, India. Row by row, I scanned the faces. It seemed the list would never end. I flicked the ball on my mouse and watched as the page moved up and new profiles occupied the screen. I looked at their pictures, one by one, and it felt like I was reading about the same child over and over again. I moved down a row and to the right when one of those photos captured my attention and my eyes locked on her face.

It was her.

Those black eyes stared back at me and pierced my heart. I felt the shock of an electrical current run through my body, just like when I was a child and electrocuted myself by pulling the vacuum plug out of the wall while it was still running. I clicked on her picture and made it bigger. There was something in her eyes, not quite determination, but I could see that this little girl had fight in her. She had a large horseshoe-shaped scar on her forehead, as if she had been branded. My heart fluttered with nervous excitement. I clicked on her profile and read the brief description about her:

"South Asia, Birthdate 05/2006 - 'M' is described by her caretakers as a quiet child. She has a history that is sensitive in nature. For further inquiry, please email."

Five? She's five? I couldn't stop staring at her picture. The longer I looked at her face, the more she captured my heart. "Sensitive in nature," what did that mean? She's five? I could not get past her age. My thoughts raced in circles, always cycling back to her age. She was so much older than a baby. How would I parent a 5-year-old? That's my starting point? I needed to clear my mind. I got up, put the leashes on the dogs, and headed out for a long walk. I needed time and space to pray.

We walked and walked and walked. After about forty minutes, we stopped and sat under the giant oak tree in the park. It was hot, and the dogs panted while they laid in the grass. I leaned against the tree, staring at the skyline, and exhaled. I didn't even know what to think anymore. Everything about this journey was nothing I would ever fathom. It had been almost a year since Nepal closed. From the outside looking in, nothing had changed. I was in the exact same spot as I was last June. I didn't have a referral for a child, and I wasn't anywhere near becoming a mom. Yet, I knew that I had changed. I was not the same person I was a year ago. My faith grew in ways I couldn't have predicted, and my view of God had undergone a subtle transformation. Little by little, the angry God of my youth was upstaged by a tender, gentle, and loving God who continued to pull and stretch me in ways I didn't know I could. I thought about everything that happened the past year. M's face kept interrupting my thoughts. "Is she the one, God? Is she?" I never dreamed I would become a first-time mom to a 5-year-old. It threw me off balance.

"Whatever you did for one of the least of these, you did it for me. Will you not do it for a 5-year-old?"

His words stabbed my heart. My body tingled at the truth He just spoke to me, and I felt the sting of humiliation. The lump in my throat grew, and I started to cry. As the tears flowed, I felt the release of my expectations, my plans, and my longing for motherhood. Sitting underneath that tree, a paradigm shifted in my heart and for the first time, I realized the truth. This was not about my desires for which child I wanted. It wasn't about me finally fulfilling my dream of motherhood, and it wasn't about me getting a baby. This was about a child who needed a mom. A child who did not have someone to hold her and comfort her. A child who didn't have someone to love her and kiss her goodnight, to sing to her as she fell asleep. It was about a child who needed a family; to know that every day she would be safe, cared for, treasured, and loved. It was about a child exchanging the title "orphan" for "daughter." It was about me stepping up to the call that God placed in my heart long ago. It was about opening my heart to become the vessel for God to bring healing and wholeness to her. A compassion and love that I had never known before, completely overwhelmed me. All I could think about was scooping her up into my arms and holding her close to my heart. A fire started to burn deep within me. She was my daughter. She was my Sofia. She was everything I wasn't looking for, and yet, she was perfectly mine. God allowed all that happened with Nepal to break my heart and make it tender for this specific child, and I knew I would do whatever it took to get her home.

I got up quickly. I practically dragged the dogs back to my house. I raced inside and refreshed my computer screen. She stared back at me. My heart felt like it was going to burst from all of the love I instantly had for her. This love was supernatural, a gift from God. Tears ran down my face as

I clicked on the link to email for more information. I filled out the inquiry form with regards to her reference number. I hit submit. In that moment, life never felt more real, and I never felt more alive.

CHAPTER 10
"M - 156"

A day went by with no response. No matter how many times I checked my email, the one I looked for continued to elude me. It had only been twenty-four hours, but it seemed like weeks. My patience was below zero, so I decided to call and find out more about "M-156." I picked up my cell phone and punched in the numbers; my heart fluttered.

"Children in Families Adoption, can I help you?"

"Hi. My name is Kristen, and I filled out an inquiry online to find out more information about one of your waiting children listed on your website. I haven't received an email, and I would really like to talk to someone about this little girl."

"Okay, if you could hold for a moment I will transfer you to our social worker who handles the waiting children. Her name is Patty."

The waiting music calmly played while my thoughts raced. I wanted to know everything there was to know about this little girl. How long has she been in the orphanage? Where is she? What is her background that is sensitive in nature?

"Hi, this is Patty," her kind voice interrupted.

"Hi Patty! My name is Kristen Williams. I filled out an online inquiry about one of your waiting children. I believe she is in India; she is listed as being in South Asia on your waiting page. I tried to wait for a response, but my eagerness got the best of me!"

"I understand. Those precious faces have a way of grabbing your heart. Do you have a home study completed?"

"I do. I was in the Nepal program and just recently officially withdrew from it." As I said those words out loud, it seemed as if all of it had happened a thousand years ago. It was a strange emotion.

"Oh, Kristen. I'm so sorry. That situation has been painful to watch unfold. So, you didn't have a referral then?" she asked.

"No. I was still waiting for the matching committee to give me one. Only recently did I realize how naive I was. I kept hoping that everything would work itself out, and that the program would reopen. Clearly, that is not the case."

"No, it isn't, unfortunately. And I don't see it reopening anytime in the near future. It's heartbreaking that those children will be stuck. I know that must have been very difficult," Patty paused, "do you feel like you are ready to move forward with a different program?"

"Well, if you would have asked me this a month ago, I wouldn't have the same answer I have today. But, yes, I am definitely ready to move forward. I have prayed and prayed about this adoption, and all I ever wanted was a healthy, baby girl. But you know what? God used the Nepal program closure to change my heart. I saw the little girl's picture on your waiting list the other day, and Patty, I can't stop thinking about her. She is so far from the child I thought I would be bringing home, but I feel strongly that she is supposed to be my daughter. I realize that might sound crazy, but I'm being completely transparent with you."

"It doesn't sound crazy at all, Kristen. I can't tell you the number of phone calls that I've had that are similar to this one. It's beautiful really, to see how families find their children. Can you give me the reference number of the little girl you saw?"

"Yes. It's M-156," I replied as excitement pulsed through my veins. I felt like a child on Christmas morning, opening the shiniest gift underneath the tree.

"Okay, give me just a moment while I pull up her file."

It seemed like an eternity for her computer to load as I anxiously tapped my foot under the table.

"AH! Munni!" she exclaimed!

"Mooney?" I asked.

"Yes! Munni! That's her name. M-u-n-n-i. Oh, Kristen, this little girl is one who tugs at my heart. In full disclosure, I will tell you that several other families have passed over her file and unmatched with her."

"What? Why? I don't understand. They were matched with her and then they stopped the adoption?" I asked.

"Yes. They had concerns about her history and how that will impact her future. The families ended up matching with other children."

I couldn't believe what I was hearing. The fire that started in my heart underneath the huge oak tree was growing. I suddenly felt very defensive for Munni and somewhat angry. "Is it really that bad? What did you mean by how it will impact her future?"

"Among other things, there are concerns for the possibility of RAD. I'm sure you learned about Reactive Attachment Disorder in your pre-adoption training, right?"

"Yes, that was included in my Hague training."

"Well, then you know it is very likely for children who have experienced extreme trauma in their early childhood to have RAD and/or other severe emotional and behavioral issues. Let's do this. I will email you her file. I want you to take some time to read through it and try to process some of it. Then, I would love for you to call me back so we can discuss this further. I will also include a doctor's evaluation and recommendation that one of the families had completed when they were reviewing her file. If you feel strongly that she is your daughter, then it's important for you to have all of the information that we have on her. If you could just give me your email address, I'll send all of this to you now. Can we reconnect in an hour or so?"

"Yes, that sounds perfect." I gave her my email address and hung up the phone. My mind was racing a million miles a second. RAD? Of all the special needs that I didn't think I could handle, RAD was at the top of the list. Are you kidding me, God? I looked at her picture, and I wouldn't accept it, not for a minute. There was something in her eyes that made me refuse to believe that she had RAD. I couldn't explain it to myself, I just knew. I refreshed my email and up popped several from Patty. My palms were sweaty as I opened the first one.

There were several pictures of Munni and in all of them, her eyes carried the same penetrating look. I quickly hit the print button and moved on to the next email. I wanted to have all of the information in front of me. After I opened all of the emails and printed the attachments, I picked up the first piece of paper to come out of my printer and started reading:

"Age of inmate at arrival of institution: 3 years"

"Describe any special needs inmate may have: Battered baby with burn scars on scalp, forehead, arms, wrists, body, and left knee..."

As I continued reading in detail about the horrendous abuse Munni had suffered, I felt nauseous and ready to vomit. I put the papers down and wept. I couldn't process any more information. My heart was broken for this precious child. Who does that? Who commits such atrocities against an innocent and vulnerable child?

I forced myself to read the rest of the information that Patty had sent me. As I did, I prayed for Munni's precious little heart. I prayed for healing and comfort and peace. I prayed for understanding, and wisdom for me to be the best mom I could be for her. I knew she was my daughter. She was my Sofia.

After about forty-five minutes, I called Patty.

"This is Patty," she answered.

"Hi." I could feel the emotion ready to burst, but quickly managed to say, "It's Kristen."

"Oh, Kristen," she responded with compassion in her voice, "I understand your heartache. This child has suffered tremendously."

"I can't even process it all, Patty," I cried, "it makes me sick to my stomach. I just want to pick her up, hug her tightly, and tell her she is loved."

"I can imagine. Kristen, there is something else you need to know. It's hard to hear but," Patty paused for a moment, and when she continued, her voice cracked. She shared details that were so horrific, I couldn't even make sense of what she was saying. Finally, she regained her composure and continued, "The amount of trauma Munni sustained is what made the other families pass. The severity of what she endured will have life-long effects. You need to be prepared for this."

I felt as if all of the oxygen left the room and nothing but a buzzing noise was in my ear. It seemed like I was dangling between reality and a parallel universe where unthinkable things happen. Anger boiled deep within my soul. At that moment, every fiber of my being was ready to fight for her. I wanted to hurt the person who did these things to her. I wanted to hit something. Rage and anguish fought against each other for my full attention and I felt desperate to get to her immediately. "Patty, she's my daughter," I cried into the phone, "and I need to get her home! What do I need to do next?"

"If you are certain you want to pursue her, we need to get your dossier switched to India. I'm the social worker, so I will put you in touch with Donna, who is the India program director. She can give you the specifics of what you will need to do to update your home study to reflect India, the immigration piece, and what all will need to be changed in your dossier. Unfortunately, she just left for vacation. However, I will flag these emails as urgent so that if she checks in while on vacation, or as soon as she gets back, she will address it immediately."

"I cannot believe the timing of this," I groaned, "I want to start on everything like, yesterday!"

"I completely understand," Patty empathized, "but you are taking the right steps. Also, I am going to send you a list of books on trauma and parenting children with trauma and children from hard places. I know you already did some training, but these books dig deeper. You will have some time on your hands, so this will be a good opportunity for you to start preparing yourself for what's ahead. It will not be easy."

"I'm an avid reader and would love a list. Patty, I will do whatever is in my power to help Munni find healing."

"Kristen, I have no doubt in my mind about that. One more thing, I found a short video of Munni. She doesn't say anything but I think you should have it. I will forward it to you now."

"A video? Oh my goodness, Patty!" I squealed. I couldn't believe that I was going to see a video of her!

"Yes. Donna took it when she was visiting the orphanage last fall. Please don't hesitate to call me if you need anything or have any other questions between now and when Donna gets back."

"I can't thank you enough, Patty!" I hung up the phone and quickly refreshed my email. There it was and in the subject line:

Video of Munni

I quickly opened the email and clicked on the YouTube link. It was forty-five seconds long. A forty-five second glimpse of my daughter. I held my breath as I pressed the play button. I gasped at the sight of her standing there in her cobalt blue, floor-length, traditional Indian dress. She took my breath away. Her head barely reached the back of the chair by which she was standing. I was surprised at how small she was. A rotating fan blew the hem of Munni's dress, causing it to ebb and flow like the ocean tide, and with each rotation, it revealed her bare feet. In the background, women were conversing in the local Indian dialect; their cadence rose above the hum of the fan. Donna's voice narrated the video, stating Munni's age and then describing the scars as she zoomed in on Munni's forehead. Munni stood like a statue, staring intently into the camera with that same penetrating glare. After about 30 seconds of Donna talking, Munni's right hand twitched ever so slightly. Anyone else probably would have missed it. I rewound and watched again. The way it twitched, she was frightened. This little girl standing in front of a stranger, trying to be so brave. As I looked into her eyes, I could see plainly now what I had missed before: fear disguised itself as anger. Tears rolled down my cheeks, and my heart spilled over with love for her. She was my daughter. She was my Sofia. I knew this in the depths of my soul as much as I knew that the sky is blue and the grass is green; I determined in that moment that I wouldn't let anything stand in the way of bringing her home.

CHAPTER 11
STUCK AGAIN - AUTUMN, 2011

I couldn't believe this was happening; it felt like a nightmare from which I could not wake. I found Sofia in June. Donna, the Indian program director, left for vacation the day I told the agency I wanted to move forward with her adoption. By the time she arrived back in the office and received my paperwork, India had suspended all new adoptions. They had a backlog of five hundred families. The suspension was supposed to be an effort to process those families through the current system and also to implement the new program under the Hague Convention requirements. In July, they stated the suspension would be in effect until September. Here I was, at the end of September, waiting for information of forward progress. Haunted by the Nepal closure and switch to Hague process, my hope deteriorated.

"I wish I had better news to share with you," Donna lamented, "but the suspension is still in effect. They are trying to get the backlogged families completed at the same time they are implementing a whole new process. They are now predicting to re-open in December."

Panic filled my chest. Tears stung my eyes. I had been praying for Sofia every single day since June 16. I mailed out picture magnets of her to those who I knew would be faithful in prayer for her. Despite reservations from some close friends and family, I knew she was my daughter. They saw an extremely troubled child with an unknown future; I saw the most beautiful little girl I had ever seen, full of fear and in need of love and nurture. Several people pulled me aside and asked if I was certain I knew what I was doing. I did not share their concerns. God made it clear to me that she was mine. This I knew in the depths of my soul. These circumstances however, left me completely helpless as

I was stuck once again. It was like the movie *"Groundhog's Day,"* where I kept reliving the same nightmare over and over again. Dread weighed me down as I wondered, *Would I ever get my daughter home?*

"The other piece that is concerning is where she is located," Donna's declaration snapped me back to the conversation. "Hyderabad is a very difficult region with which to work. It was closed to adoptions for years due to child trafficking, and only recently re-opened. We have been trying to assess what the process will look like since parents have to attend court. We are leaning towards making it a two-trip process because the time between attending court and then actually receiving the written court order and passport is quite extensive. You're talking about a two to three month gap."

I felt like someone punched me in the stomach. At every turn, bad news confronted me. I battled against my thoughts and tried to stay positive. "Okay, so what can I do between now and December so that as soon as they re-open, I can be matched with her? Also, when should I send in my first payment?"

"Unfortunately, there is really nothing you can do. India is unpredictable and Hyderabad even more so. It's imperative that all of your documents are dated according to the timelines that India requires. We don't know what that will look like until they re-open. It would be a waste of time and money for you to complete anything now because it is most likely that you would have to redo them once the program is up and running. We don't want to risk you having documents that are dated before the Hague transition is in effect."

"I hate this," I spewed, "I just want her home. Do you want me to send the first payment? I don't want anything on my end to be a holdup."

"I'm so sorry, Kristen. I know this isn't the news you were hoping for, and in regards to the payment, I think it's best for you to wait. We can't do anything now anyway, so it's better for you to have it. This is a tricky situation because you are dealing with two complicated processes simultaneously; the new Hague transition and Hyderabad. We will be doing everything on our end to keep you informed. Again, my apologies. I understand how emotional this process is," Donna consoled.

I hung up the phone. I sat in silence. I didn't even know what to think anymore. Once more, I had no idea how, if, or when my daughter would come home. In addition, there had been zero movement in the Congo process. I was holding steady at number seventeen. Never in my life had I felt so lost and adrift in a giant abyss of the unknown.

CHAPTER 12
NOVEMBER 14, 2011

The last student left the classroom. It was time for lunch, and I sat down to quickly check my email before heading to the teacher's lounge. Up popped an email from Donna with the subject title "Hold." My heart raced and my thoughts ran wild. Joy took over as I excitedly opened the email. After months and months of waiting, was she finally able to place Munni on hold for me?

> Hi Kristen,
> In looking at the lack of communication from Hyderabad, I am putting our waiting children from Hyderabad on hold formally. I am visiting them in January and we'll see if that can jumpstart anything. If after the visit it appears we can get it going, I'll get in touch with you, but wanted you to know how things are. Wish I had better news.
>
> All the best,
> Donna

I sat in stunned silence staring at the screen. A lump grew in my throat, and I could feel tears trying to break free from their confinement.

"Hey! Are you ready to eat?" my colleague Catie startled me from my state of shock.

I swallowed down my heartbreak and smiled, "Yep! I'm starved." I got up, walked out of my classroom, and went on with the day as if nothing had happened. Except, everything had happened. Once again, my whole world felt flipped and off-center. Nothing made sense, and I floundered in the confusion of it all.

CHAPTER 13
DECEMBER, 2011 - TURNING POINT

I hadn't said a word about the email from Donna. Two weeks prior to receiving it, I attended a Christian conference. One of the speakers shared about her battle with infertility and how for two decades, she wrestled with God because she knew in her heart she was supposed to be a mom. She talked about the depths of despair she felt during the wait and how she clung to His promises. In the end, she adopted twins. Her story resonated deep within me. My spirit stirred as she spoke. One thing she said stayed with me. She talked about how she refused to give life to negativity during her wait. She said she never spoke out her fears of never becoming a mom because she did not want to breathe life into those negative thoughts. When I read Donna's email, the speaker's words flooded my mind, and I determined that I would not speak of that email. I wouldn't share it on my blog. I wouldn't share it with my family. I wouldn't share it with my friends. I would not give life to the news Donna gave me. However, despite my best efforts to remain positive, I could not stop the despair that quickly filled my heart. It found cracks in my faith as water seeps through the fissures of a foundation, and it flooded my spirit with doubt, fear, and desperation.

Once again, December 12 loomed over me. The closer it came, the deeper I spiraled into heartache. I thought back to almost two years prior when I was convinced I heard God whisper a due date to me and I felt ashamed. How could I have been so foolish? All I did was set myself up for devastation. A crushing weight constantly pressed against my heart, I could not free myself from this dark pit of despair. I hated everything I felt.

I woke up and immediately the knot in my stomach tightened. It arrived. December 12 was here and Sofia was not. What was worse, she now had a face. I knew parts of her story. I prayed for her every single day, and I felt with every ounce of my being that she was my daughter. But the latest email from Donna filled me with such trepidation; it seemed an impossible feat that she would ever come home.

I got out of bed to reluctantly start my day. It felt like cement blocks weighted my every step. I prayed for God's peace; it never came. I made myself a pot of coffee and determined I would live this day in faith. I sat down to have my prayer time and opened my bible to the book of psalms: my refuge when I'm overwhelmed to the point of paralysis. I tried to read the words, but they kept running away from me. A weight pulled from deep within, and it sucked me into a vacuum of fear. Terrified that if I turned around, I would face the truth that Sofia was never coming home. I looked out my front window and the tears started to fall. I silently begged God to please, please bring her home. The longer I prayed, the tears turned to sobs, and within minutes, I was heaving with grief and heartbreak as I tried to elude the one thing I had yet to acknowledge. The thing I didn't want to face. The obstacle I tried to avoid and the weight that kept me from experiencing the etherealness of God's peace. He gently, but firmly pressed upon my spirit, and I could no longer resist against what He had been calling me to do all along: surrender.

I fell to the floor and wept. Groans escaped from deep within my soul and with them, every piece of my dream followed. My heart burned like fire; as I lay crying on my living room floor, I watched the embers of my one true desire rise up and evaporate. I could hardly breathe; the lump in my throat impeded my voice so I silently prayed, "Take her, Jesus. If there is a family who is better for her than me, let her go to them." I did it. I released her to Him. As I left her on the altar, a watershed of sorrow poured out from me. Tears soaked my carpet. Simon came over to me and gently licked my face. I have no idea how long I laid there; my grieving eventually turned into sleep.

* * * * *

I had nothing left. The day before, I reached my lowest of low and surrendered Sofia to God. Today, I walked in this weird state of being - no longer weighed down by fear, but also not lifted by hope. It felt gross. Searching for a distraction, I checked my email. Mindlessly scrolling through stupid spam, I almost missed it. A new comment on one of my blog posts from November. I clicked and opened it.

Hi Kristen -- I recently found your blog. I wonder, are you using CIFA and is your Sofia in HYD by any chance? If so, I'd love to connect. Blessings, Sarah

My heart skipped a beat. I clicked on her profile and the link to her blog. I started reading. I couldn't believe it! Another Indian adoption blog! And, someone who is also adopting from Hyderabad! What were the chances? For months I scoured the web for Indian adoption blogs and only found one other blog, but their girls were already home. With this new email, I felt like I hit the jackpot. I wrote a quick email introducing myself and prayed she would respond. My thoughts raced to yesterday; with all of my being, I let her go. I relinquished her to His will, to the best family He had in store for her, whether that was me or someone else. I loved her so much; it was the hardest thing He asked me to do. Reading this comment on my blog felt like a shot of adrenaline to my adoption journey.

I went on with my day, checking my email frequently; I was on pins and needles waiting for her to reply. Finally, several hours later, I received a response. I tore into the email like a bag of candy on Easter morning. Every sentence I read brought a bigger smile to my face. She was using the same agency as me, and her daughter used to be in Sofia's orphanage, but was transferred to an NGO orphanage. She told me that her best friend, Meredith, was also adopting a little girl from Hyderabad. She and Meredith were neighbors. They signed on with the agency before the suspension, a month before I found Sofia. I couldn't believe all of the information she had. I sat back in my chair and thanked God. I felt such peace. Maybe God wanted Sofia with me after all.

The next day I received an email from Meredith. We exchanged several emails and found we had much in common. We talked about the adoptions, our dogs, our faith, traveling, and photography. I couldn't believe how easily a friendship blossomed between us. She told me that Sarah had a call scheduled with Donna for later that day. I agreed to be in prayer about the phone call, and hoped for developments in all three of our adoptions. She said they would be in touch to fill me in on what transpired.

I found that I began to live my life in increments of waiting. I guess it had always been there; I just didn't realize it. The adoption process highlighted the pattern of doing, then waiting. Early evening, I received the email from Sarah. She told me she had a back up plan. I felt myself grinning from ear to ear. She said she had been in contact with another agency, one who had an established relationship with the orphanage in Hyderabad. They worked with them for years. The agency told Sarah they were confident they could bring our girls home. She also told me about a massive database India had been creating in order to streamline the adoption process. Up until this point, agencies worked directly with orphanages. The orphanages let the agencies know about the children who were available. In addition, the agencies would send their representative to visit the orphanages, meet the children, take pictures, and collect more information to share with prospective parents. That's how Donna was able to get the video of Sofia. This new database would somewhat eliminate that orphanage-agency relationship. The goal of the database was for every orphanage to list their available children so that every agency licensed in India had access to all of the available children's files. In theory, it sounded amazing. It sounded like a win for these children. More exposure to help find them families. In reality, it seemed a daunting task. Sarah said this new database project was partly responsible for the suspension being continued past September. She added that Donna planned to visit Hyderabad in January to see if an in-person visit could stir up movement in the adoption process. I thought back to the email Donna sent me in November, telling me of her plan to visit in January. Sarah suggested if Donna's trip wasn't successful, that we switch to the other agency. Either way, it seemed our girls would be coming home.

I got up and danced around. I grabbed Simon and hugged him. "She's coming home, Mister!" Happiness pulsated through me and I couldn't stop smiling. I thanked God for His faithfulness. He brought me to the point of total surrender with the purpose of building my faith. Would I one hundred percent, absolutely and completely, trust Him? He led me to a deeper level of intimacy by surrendering her to Him; through that surrender, He tore my faith muscle. But without that tear, I would not experience growth. I felt as the tear healed, so my faith increased.

* * * * *

Ever since I connected with Sarah and Meredith, new hope took residence in my heart. I found myself excited for Christmas. I had feared the season would be permanently ruined for me. Even though I was back in the waiting game, this time it was different. It was different because I had hope.

I bought a tree and decorated it. I put up my outdoor lights and truly enjoyed the days leading up to Christmas. I still had some last minute gifts to buy, but I decided I would take care of it on December 21, my first day of the Christmas break.

I pulled into the parking lot and parked my car. Snow gently fell. I smiled. I couldn't believe how things had turned around. School was out, the break started, and I was full of renewed faith. I had a few quick things I wanted to buy and knew I could be in and out quickly. I decided to check my email before I went into the store. There was an email from Sarah with the subject: Journeys of Adoption. I quickly clicked on it and began reading:

Hi Kristen,

I just spoke with Heather at Journeys of Adoption (the other adoption agency). I was asking her about your situation and she suggested that you call her (today or tomorrow if you can). On Jan. 1st all of the children in India who are available for international adoption are supposed to go on a database, where all agencies will be able to access their information. Any agency then, can request a child's file (so, for example, Munni's file could go to another agency for another family). JOA is trying to match particular children with families before that happens. Since you are not officially a client of CIFA, your situation is different than ours and it may be better for you to simply go with JOA right away, rather than waiting for Donna to go to India. Does this make sense? Let me know if it doesn't and I can try to explain it better. Feel free to call me if that's easier.

When you call JOA, ask for Heather, she can let you know if it's possible for them to help you.

Blessings to you,
Sarah

My heart quickened, and my eyes filled with tears as I scrolled for Sarah's number.

"Hi, Kristen," her voice soothed. "Did my email make sense?"

"Kind of. Does that mean someone else could match with Munni come January 1? For example, if a family already has their paperwork in?"

"Well, technically yes. But, that's where things are unclear because of the suspension. India hasn't been accepting new families as you know, so the agencies are expecting it to be chaos when the database goes live. No one really knows how it's going to function in reality. I spoke to Heather for a long time today. She knows about you and your situation and feels confident that JOA can help you. They will be out of the office for the Christmas break though, so I really think you should call her today."

"I feel sick," I squeaked out through the lump in my throat.

"I understand, Kristen. The Lord knows your heart for sweet Munni. I believe he is directing your steps. I am praying for you in this and praying for Munni. I'm going to let you go so you can call Heather. Please email me or call me, whatever is easier for you, and let me know what she says."

"I will. I can't thank you enough, Sarah. Honestly. I know God crossed our paths for a reason, and I, too, believe that we are seeing it being played out right now before our very eyes. But, I'm scared."

"That's understandable. Meredith and I will be praying. Go, call Heather!"

"Thank you!"

I hung up the phone and stared out my windshield at the falling snow. *Lord, what are you doing?* I silently prayed. I fought the confusion and fear that battled to fill my heart. I started my car and drove home as fast as I could. I wanted to have all of my paperwork in front of me when I made the telephone call to the agency; I was not going to be responsible for any delay. I got home in record time, parked my car, and ran inside my house. Once I had my adoption file in front of me, I quickly searched for JOA's number and called it.

"Journeys of Adoption," a kind voice answered.

"Hi, may I speak with Heather?" I inquired.

"Sure, just one moment." As she placed me on hold and subtle background music filled the void.

"This is Heather."

"Hi, Heather. My name is Kristen. My friend Sarah called you earlier today," I managed to get out before my voice started to crack, "and I'm really hoping you can help me get my daughter home from India." I finished through sobs I no longer could contain.

"Oh! I was hoping I would hear from you today. It's okay. Take a deep breath," she said calmly. Her steady demeanor was the oxygen mask I needed. "Let me explain some things to you that I explained to Sarah," she continued in her confident voice. "We have a long-standing relationship with this specific orphanage. So, even though Hyderabad is a difficult region with which to work, because of our relationship with the staff there, we are confident that we can help you bring Munni home. In fact, I'm also adopting a little girl who is in the same orphanage as Munni."

"No way!"

"Yes!" she exclaimed, "and we just had two other families recently come home with their daughters who are also from the same orphanage. Now, I have to warn you: it will not be an easy, quick process, so you need to be prepared for that. But she will come home."

"You have no idea," I lamented. "Nothing about my process has been quick or easy."

"Well, then, this sounds like it should be par for course," Heather acknowledged.

"Pretty much!" I laughed, "I realize that it's going to be a battle to get her home. I'm ready to fight. I just want to make sure that you think for sure that your agency can get her home? I don't know how much Sarah told you about my story, but I found Munni on another agency's waiting list. First, the caseworker was on vacation when I found her, and then the stupid suspension went into effect before my dossier was able to be switched over from Nepal to India. It's literally been one roadblock after another," I ranted.

"We can get her home," Heather declared with assured confidence.

Her words danced into my thoughts and shattered the remaining pieces of protective barrier guarding me from ultimate heartbreak. My face crumpled. Like a sudden rainstorm, the tears came hard and fast. Somehow, I managed to squeak out, "I can't believe it! I can't believe it!"

"Well, you better believe it! However, we do need to work quickly. The new database will be going into effect in January. We are trying to match families with children ahead of the database going live so that Munni will never be on the database, if that makes sense. There is still much confusion surrounding how this whole new process is going to work and there are many questions that still don't have answers," Heather informed me.

"How long do you think this whole process will take?" I asked.

"That's the million dollar question," Heather laughed. "I was matched with my daughter last March, and there is no end in sight. Now, granted, the suspension really put a wrench in things so that complicated the timeline. I would say eighteen months would be on the quicker side of things, and two years would be on the normal side of the timeline."

"Wow," I sat there stunned. Two years. My heart broke and I felt sick thinking about her having to wait in the orphanage for two more years. "You don't think there is any way it could be faster?"

"Kristen, it's Hyderabad," Heather reminded me.

"I have a feeling I'm going to hear this sentence a lot in the coming months," I replied.

"Unfortunately," she responded.

"Okay. So, I have another question. Do you think there is any way that I could get an updated picture of Munni? The last picture I have of her is from the other caseworker's trip to India, which was in October of 2010.

"Well, when families travel, they are usually able to take pictures for the other families who are still waiting. We do have a family who will be traveling soon. I'm sure they will be more than happy to take some pictures of Munni for you."

"Munni has a very specific scar on her forehead; it almost looks like a horseshoe," I described.

"Wait a minute," Heather paused, "I think your daughter is in my daughter's referral picture. I've always thought it was strange because they are not supposed to have multiple children in referral pictures unless they are siblings. This picture is from September 2009. What is your email? I'll send it to you now and you can tell me if it's your Munni."

My heart raced as I quickly told her my email address and waited expectantly for hers to pop up in my inbox.

SUBJECT: Munni?

I couldn't open the attachment fast enough, and my computer apathetically downloaded it as slowly as possible. I waited in agony as the picture lethargically materialized from the top of the screen. Little by little, more of the photograph revealed itself. A hot pink sari. A tiny, little head with short, black hair. And then, as the pixels clarified and moved further down onto the forehead, there it was.

The horseshoe.

I let out a gasp.

"Is it her?" Heather asked in eager anticipation.

"Yes!" I cried through tears of joy. I couldn't believe it. As the picture continued to download and the rest of her beautiful face came into view, I sat back in my chair and cried in total disbelief. How in the world did this happen? She had only been in the orphanage for three months when this picture was taken.

"HEATHER! Do you understand what's going on here?" I was freaking out! "I can't believe this! When I started this adoption journey I wanted a perfect, healthy little baby. I signed up for the Nepal program. And then, just when I was ready to be matched, the U.S. Government shut down the program. Of course, I was devastated. But, God used that time to change my heart and got me to a point of being open to special needs adoption and brought me back to India, the place from where I originally wanted to adopt. Last June, I found Munni on CIFA's waiting list. I tried to move forward with her, but the caseworker was gone on vacation, and by time she got back and could send my dossier, India implemented the suspension. So, I waited and waited and waited. Then, in November, Donna sent me an email telling me that she was putting their Hyderabad program on hold because the region was too difficult."

"Wow," Heather replied.

"Right? But, then Sarah randomly found my blog. I never told anyone about the email that Donna sent me. Sarah just happened to call you one day and mention me and my situation. Then, she emailed me and told me what she found out from you about what your agency can do. Well, one thing led to another, and here we are having this conversation. You just sent me that picture of our daughters. Munni had only been in the orphanage three months when that photo was taken, and somehow, she managed to get into the background of the referral picture of your daughter's picture. Heather! I know you are supposed to be my caseworker. I don't believe for one second that this is just a coincidence." I was fully crying at this point, "God brought me to your agency, and this is a total confirmation. Things like this don't just happen."

"I'm completely stunned," Heather proclaimed. "And I had no idea how intricate your story was! This is pretty incredible."

"Ahhhhhhh! I am so happy right now."

"Well, let's keep your momentum rolling. I'm going to have my assistant send you a bunch of emails. It will come in a series and will include the contract and everything pertaining to the Indian adoption program. Also, if you could please have your home study agency send me a draft of your home study, that way we can get started on the review because there will be some edits that will have to be done in order to reflect India and what they require. First, if you could fill out the application, scan, and email that back to us, it will get the ball rolling."

"Okay. I'm on my Christmas break, so this is perfect timing for me to tackle this!"

"Great! Ready to bring your girl home?"

"You have no idea!"

Chapter 14
December 2011

Sitting in the salon chair, looking at my foil-filled space hair, waiting for the highlights to finish processing, I couldn't help but smile ear to ear. The shock still hadn't worn off; Sofia was coming home! From the second I sat down, the words came tumbling out as I recounted the whole story to Molly, my hair stylist. Cloud nine didn't even come close to describe the joy that overwhelmed me. I sat there fantasizing about the moment we would finally meet. Looking into her dark, black eyes, would I find a hint of love staring back at me? My cellphone shook me from my reverie. I recognized the number immediately and quickly answered, "Hello?"

"Hi, is this Kristen?"

"This is she," I replied.

"Hey, this is Heather at Journeys. Um, I'm looking over your application and I see it says that you are in a concurrent adoption with the Congo. You never mentioned this in our conversation."

"Oh. Well, it never came up because I guess I was just so focused on Munni. When I was in the Nepal program and the U.S. Department of State suspended the adoptions, I started the Congo adoption because my agency told me that it was an option that many families were doing since they didn't know how long the suspension would last."

"Well, India doesn't allow concurrent adoptions," Heather informed me.

Once again, reality started spinning and my stomach tightened. "I don't even have a referral." I blurted out. Tears welled in my eyes, spilling over. "I won't lose her, Heather!" my voice cracked. Two ladies sitting next to me turned to see the commotion. "I can't lose her! I will stop my Congo adoption. I will do whatever it takes!" I continued my pleading through sobs.

"I'm not necessarily saying you have to stop your Congo adoption, but you will have to sign an agreement that you won't accept a referral until after Munni is home. That could potentially be two years from now. This is the only way that we will be able to make this happen."

My heart beating rapidly, fear once again fought to fill my entire being. "I will do whatever it takes," I proclaimed, "I will not lose her. She is my daughter, Heather! I'm not losing her!" I cried, "I didn't get this far, hit every road block imaginable, finally find an agency who can bring her home, just to lose her. That's not going to happen!" The fight raged within me. And in a moment that felt like a twisted, deranged, childhood fable, I sacrificed my non-existent Congolese child for the daughter whose face sent an electrical current through my body - a message from heaven that signaled the beginning of the process that would weave our lives together.

* * * * *

I recovered from the near fatal blow of the concurrent adoption fiasco and managed to enjoy Christmas. I told my family about the progress that had been made with Sofia's adoption process. While they seemed happy for me, she was not included in the Christmas prayer. In fact, she wasn't mentioned at all that day. I left my mom's Christmas night feeling the sting in my heart and wondered; if I had been expecting a child the traditional way at Christmas, would the enthusiasm been different? In addition, I received all of the contracts, fees, and placing agreements from the agency and had a mild heart attack when I saw the amount needed to get everything started. I had some of the money saved that would cover the application fees and home study review. I was also able to negotiate the removal of the education fee since I had completed that for the Hague portion of my Nepal home study, but I still needed a whopping four thousand dollars for the first agency fee. I didn't have anything close to that. I'm not sure what came over me, but somehow I mustered the courage to ask my dad if he could help me. Instead of a direct no, he surprised me and told me to gather all of my financial documents and bring them over so we could discuss it.

In addition to my poor relationship choices, my past plagued me with horrible financial decisions as well. Those weren't easy to bounce back from either, but I'd been working hard for that last several years trying to right the ship. Even though my mistakes were from many years prior, the tentacles from their consequences stretched long and deep. I attended the Dave Ramsey Financial Peace University a few years ago and implemented his tactics ever since. I didn't have any open credit cards, and I worked a second job slinging pizza. Little by little, I chipped away at the stupid financial debt mountain I had created. When I lost the money from my 403b in the Nepal adoption, my dad never said it out loud, but was quick to make sighs and groans any time it was mentioned. His disapproval was clear. So now that he was willing to go over my financial information, it gave me a small spark of hope.

As I pulled up to their driveway, all my fears escalated and I thought back to the first night I announced my adoption plans. My dad's initial response included his obvious disdain and very clear directive not to expect any help from him. I wondered if I should just go home. I exhaled and sat there. I literally had no other options. I silently prayed for God to soften my dad's heart. I took a deep breath, swallowed my pride, grabbed my folder, got out of my car, and walked into my financial audit.

"Hi, Honey!" my mom greeted me cheerily as I walked in the door.

"Hi, Mom."

"Do you want something to eat?" she asked.

"No thanks. My stomach is in knots. Where's Dad?"

"He's in the T.V. Room." She gave a hopeful glance in the direction of where the impending decision awaited me.

My heart accelerated and I breathed in. I walked around the corner into my dad's "office." He was watching the news channel and looked up when he saw me.

"Hey, Dad."

"Hi, Kris," the name only my dad called me. "How are you?"

"I'm good."

"These politicians are so stupid." His classic conversation starter.

"It's always something, Dad," I offered.

"Ha! Isn't that the truth."

I felt like we might be off to a neutral start. I held my breath.

"Well, did you bring over your paperwork?" he asked.

"Yep. It's all right here. You know I did the Dave Ramsey plan and I've been working on it since November, 2007."

He took the folder and slowly leafed through all of my documents that I had meticulously organized by each account to show progress. "You made stupid mistakes. What were you thinking?" He growled as he launched his attack and began to eviscerate every single financial mistake I had ever made. His disapproval spewed out like venom. He finished his torture session with his verdict: "I'm not going to help you."

I staggered and felt my face getting hot. He delivered it so blunt and matter-of-fact. I wondered why he even bothered to have me bring my documents over in the first place. Once I regained my balance from the initial left hook that blindsided me, I retaliated with my own upper cut, "Is that what you said to Uncle Robert when you helped him with his divorce from crazy Wendy? Did you tell him how stupid he was for marrying her in the first place?" My momentum started, and I wasn't going to stop. All I could think about was Sofia. "All I've ever wanted my entire life, Dad, was to be a mom!" I could feel the tears coming, but I wasn't stopping, "You spent thousands and thousands and thousands of dollars on that stupid divorce, and I'm asking you to help me bring my daughter home! You haven't even asked ONCE to see her picture!" By this time, tears were streaming down my face and I could no longer control my sobs. I dug her picture out of my purse in an attempt to show him her face.

"I don't want to see her picture." My dad surprised me as he held his hand up to shield his face from it.

"Why?" I asked in disbelief.

"I don't want to get attached!" he yelled at me.

"I'M ALREADY ATTACHED!" I screamed through my tears.

My dad stared back at me and repeated his verdict, "I'm not going to help you, and that's that."

I glared at my dad in total disbelief. Anger boiled in my heart, and flames shot out of my eyes. I couldn't even speak to him. I grabbed my papers and ran past my mom, who at this point, had been standing in the doorway when our voices amplified into a shouting match. I could hear her calling my name as I bolted out the front door, but I didn't stop. I got into my car and drove off as fast as I could. I have no idea how I made it home. I could barely see through the tears.

* * * * *

Three days passed since the war with my dad. Any hope of bringing Sofia home had completely vanished. I slipped into a major depression. If not for my dogs, I wouldn't have moved from my couch. Empty wine bottles and crumpled up tissues littered my living room floor. My hair matted to my head, I was still wearing the same clothes I wore that day. I didn't return texts or answer calls. I hit rock bottom. I spent three days crying out to God, begging Him to give me an answer. I felt like I was a constant yo-yo and for the life of me, could not understand His purpose. At every turn, there seemed to be a battle. Every time I reached a breakthrough, I slammed into another roadblock. This time, however, it wasn't a roadblock. It was a giant brick wall. And to make matters worse, the lies from my childhood religion began to scream in my head. How worthless I was. What a fool to believe that God would ever love me enough to entrust me to be Sofia's mom. With my track record, those lies were beginning to resemble the truth.

My dogs started barking, startling me from my melancholy. Someone was at my door. What the heck? Annoyed, I got up from my heavyhearted prison to see who could possibly be on my front porch. I opened my front door and saw her face. I immediately started bawling.

"What the hell is going on in here?" she asked as she hugged me and pushed the door all the way open, surveying the physical evidence of my emotional breakdown.

"I lost her," I sobbed into my best friend's shoulder.

"What are you talking about? I thought the agency said they could bring her home? Seriously, what the hell? Kristen! What is going on?" Janet asked concerned as she looked around at the state of my house. "You know I'm only in town for a week and you peaced-out on me and stopped replying to my texts. I'm worried about you. What is going on? What do you mean you lost her?"

We sat down on the couch, and I started to explain. "I need four thousand dollars to start her adoption. I don't have that money. Somehow, I got the courage to ask my dad."

Janet's eyes widened.

"I know. It was a big deal. He told me to get all of my paperwork together and bring it over to his house. You know I've been working so hard, Janet," I started crying, "to fix all the stupid mistakes I've made. I feel like I'll never stop paying for my mistakes," I wailed.

"What did your dad say?"

"He said he wouldn't help me."

"Even after you showed him all of your paperwork?"

"Yes. I'm having a hard time not hating him right now."

"You can't hate him. He's your dad," Janet replied.

"I know. But I'm SO MAD at him," I seethed through gritted teeth, "and I told him that I couldn't believe that he gave my uncle thousands and thousands of dollars to pay for his stupid divorce, but wouldn't help his own daughter with her adoption."

"What did he say when you told him that?"

"He just kept saying that he wasn't going to help me. It's like a giant summary of my entire childhood. He was never there for me emotionally, for the things that were most important to me. You know that I played soccer from kindergarten through high school. I played select, and our team traveled. Think about all those games, Janet. Do you know that he only came to half of one game? It was my junior year in high school. I remember I saw him coming through the gate and my heart almost came out of my chest. I couldn't believe it! Finally! He came to see me play! And he didn't even stay to watch the whole game."

Janet looked at me with compassion in her eyes.

"And you know what else?" I asked her. "He wouldn't even look at Sofia's picture." My voice cracked. I cried even harder.

"Whaaat? Why?"

"He said he didn't want to get attached."

"Oh. Well, maybe because of what happened with Nepal," Janet offered.

"I don't care!" I wailed.

"I'm not saying he's right for not looking at her picture," Janet quickly responded. "Just that maybe he has more feelings than he's letting on."

"Well, he doesn't have to worry about those feelings because she's not coming home. Ever. At the beginning of December, God brought me to a place of total surrender and I did, Janet. I gave her to Him. I told Him that if He had a better family for her than me, then I wanted her to go to them, no matter how painful that was for me. That was SO hard for me to do. But I did it. And the next day is when Sarah contacted me. So I thought that maybe God was saying that she is supposed to be with me. But now, with this, it seems like it's a giant *No!* A complete and total dead end. I have no money. I spent all of my 403b on stupid Nepal. Even if I worked a double every day between now and when the new database goes live, there is no way I can get four thousand dollars. She's gone." I stared out my window and crumpled into a heaving ball of sobs.

Janet sat in silence watching me cry.

I felt sick and hopeless and full of the deepest sadness I had ever felt in my entire life.

"No."

"What?"

"NO!" Janet repeated with authority.

"What do you mean?" I asked.

"I mean, NO! This is not how this ends."

"I don't have any money, Janet," I whined.

"I don't care," she stated. "Almost every single day since June, I've heard you tell me how Sofia is your daughter. I've heard the love in your voice, Kristen. The way you talk about her. The look on your face just when you say her name. She is your daughter. And anyone else who has seen and heard it would tell you the same thing. You have prayed for her every day. You just told me that you surrendered her to God and the very next day is when Sarah contacted you, right?"

"Yeah," I responded, "——but, now—— "

"But nothing," Janet interrupted. "Maybe God is waiting for you to fight for her. You told me that you would do whatever it takes to get her home. So, do whatever it takes!" Janet challenged me.

"I don't know what to do!" I cried, "I don't have any money."

"What about that grant you won in the summer?"

"That grant is for the Congo," I replied.

"Well, that's not happening for awhile, so why don't you call them and ask if you can use it for Sofia?"

"I don't know if it works like that," I tentatively replied.

"Where is your fight?" Janet demanded. "What happened to the Kristen who couldn't wait to show me Sofia's picture? Where is the Kristen who told me last summer that she knew as much as the sky is blue that Sofia is your daughter? Where is the Kristen that told me that you pray for her every single day, all day long? Where is the Kristen who told me that you would fight with all that you are to bring her home? Find THAT Kristen and bring her back here to fight for Sofia. Fight for YOUR daughter. Fight for YOUR SOFIA, and make that phone call, and get YOUR daughter HOME!"

I stared at Janet stunned by her call to action. "Did you just go all drill sergeant on me?" I asked her, laughing through my tears.

"Not even close."

"I love you so much," I told her as I hugged her, "Seriously, I am so lucky to have you as my best-friend. Thanks for kicking my ass when I need it."

"I love you, too," She responded. "And you better call them tomorrow," she warned me.

"I will! I fear your wrath. You're scary when you go Army!" I joked.

"Get up and go splash water on your face. Put on a baseball hat and let's get a drink. I'm not letting you sit in this tissue blizzard any longer," she said as she looked around at my living room floor, covered in tear-stained tissue balls.

*   *   *   *   *

I woke up the next morning with renewed fight. I made coffee and sat down to have my prayer time. Whatever was going to happen with the phone call in regards to the grant, I wanted my focus to be centered on Christ. If the grant wouldn't be the vessel to start this adoption, I had to believe that somehow, someway, God had a plan. I opened my Bible to the Old Testament. I never used to read the old testament, but this adoption journey brought a new appreciation for it. I found a kindred alliance with the Jews as I found myself relating to much of their faith journey while I stumbled along on mine. It seemed God would just finish pulling off a spectacular miracle when their grumbling would immediately begin about some new problem. It was as if they had already forgotten the feat he had just accomplished. I saw myself so much in those pages. I imagined myself on the banks of the Red Sea, the Egyptian army hot on our tail, looking across the water, fearing certain death, and definitely seeing no way out. When suddenly, the waters part, creating an incredible pathway to the other side! Whoa! And just when the last Hebrew makes it over, the water walls collapse, swallowing up the Egyptian army with it. No sooner had that happened, their stomachs started to growl. Everyone was hungry. Oh man. They're in the middle of the desert. Where in the world are they going to get food? Everyone starts freaking out. They can't imagine where or how they will eat, even though they just walked through the middle of the Red Sea. I can relate to these people! It seemed that every time a new obstacle came my way, I easily forgot how God previously provided the way out.

I turned to Genesis and began reading about Sarah and Abraham. I could somewhat empathize with Sarah. I waited a long time to become a mom; motherhood felt like the carrot that would forever be dangled in front of me. She laughed when the angel promised her a son in her old age. I understood her scoffing. After all those years and all those supplications, would the answered prayer finally come in her geriatric years? That seemed impossible. And then God called her on it, asked why she laughed. I was reading along taking note in my head, thinking, *I don't know that I wouldn't have laughed too, if I were Sarah. Being that old? Praying for all those years?* I sat there and reflected on my own journey, all of the twists and turns it had taken. It was definitely nothing I ever would have anticipated. I continued reading and the next verse stopped me in my tracks. A tingling sensation took over my body.

Is anything too hard for the Lord? [3]

I held my breath and prayed. "Is that you, Lord?"

Make The Call

I trembled and began crying. Emotions flooded me. I didn't know what to do first. I stood up and got my adoption file box and pulled out my grant folder. I found the official grant acceptance letter and the phone number for Becky. My hands wouldn't stop shaking as I punched in the numbers. The phone rang on the other end.

"Good morning, Help Us Adopt," a woman answered.

"Hi, I am a grant recipient and I was hoping to speak with Becky about my grant," I tried to sound breezy even though I was certain the woman could hear my heart pounding through the phone.

"Sure. She just happens to be in the office this morning. Let me see if she is on the other line. Can you hold for just one moment?" she asked.

"Of course," I answered as I thought about the coincidence of her being in the office. My nerves were in overdrive and I thought I might throw up or have diarrhea. My body hadn't decided which one.

"This is Becky," her pleasant voice snapped me back to attention.

"Hi, Becky. This is Kristen and I won your June grant." I attempted to sound upbeat, happy, and most of all, put-together. But the words that came out next made my facade come tumbling down like a Jenga tower. "When you called me last June to let me know I won the grant, I withdrew from the Nepal program the day we spoke," my voice cracked, "and you told me my daughter wasn't in Nepal," a deluge of sobs and tears punctuated my sentence.

"Kristen! I remember. I told you I didn't know where she was, but I knew you would find her. Did you find her?"

The lump in my throat was so tight I could hardly breathe. "Yes," a high-pitched voice that didn't sound like myself replied, "in India."

"Oh, that's wonderful!" Becky exclaimed.

I took a deep breath and somewhat recomposed myself before I continued, "That's why I'm calling you. I need four thousand dollars to start her adoption. Becky, I found her one week after we hung up the phone," as I proceeded to tell her all of the twists and turns that happened in the six months since we had last talked.

"Wow! Kristen, this is incredible. I'm floored." Becky responded.

"So, my question is, am I allowed to use the three thousand five hundred dollar grant for Sofia even though when I applied, it was for the Congo?"

"The grant is yours. You send me your agency information and we will wire the money. Kristen, go get your daughter!"

"Oh my gosh, Becky!" I wept and fell to my knees, "I can't thank you enough! You have no idea!" I cried on my living room floor. "You have no idea!" I repeated once again in total disbelief and overcome with emotion. "I don't have enough words to express how thankful I am, Becky." I managed through a squeaky voice that heaved with emotion.

"It's my pleasure! This is why we do what we do. Email me that information so we can get this ball rolling. And please send us a picture when you get your precious daughter home!"

CHAPTER 15
MOVING FORWARD

Several weeks passed and I was still in shock that Sofia's adoption was actually happening. The first set of fees were paid, thanks to the grant from Help Us Adopt. On January 20, India launched the brand new database. They only accepted one hundred prospective adoptive parents for registration each month, so if I didn't get a slot in January, my agency would have to try again in February. Thankfully, my agency got me registered. Because the database was new, in addition to making the program Hague compliant, not all of the pieces were functioning in the capacity for which they were designed. Sofia was listed as special needs. The special needs portion of the database was not operational; so while I was registered, I had yet to be officially matched with her. Deep down, fear and panic continued to taunt me as I secretly wondered if that day would ever come. It was a daily battle to fight back against those emotions.

I barely spoke to my dad since our blowout in December. The feelings were too raw. His open disdain for my adoption, and his blatant refusal to help me with my deepest desire inadvertently ruptured the childhood wounds I had worked so diligently to bury. My mom, on the other hand, rejoiced with me when I told her about the grant being applied to Sofia's adoption fees. She cheered me on in my pursuit of my daughter and quietly prayed for restoration between my dad and me. I continued working as many extra shifts as possible at the pizzeria in addition to my teaching job. Even though I knew there was no way I could ever come up with the whole amount for her adoption, I knew I needed to put in as much effort as I was able. I also persisted with my search for grant organizations that didn't discriminate against singles. That, in and of itself, was a mighty feat.

As the winter days came and went, a new obsession took over me. I checked my email relentlessly, hoping to see the notification of the approval from India. That approval would allow me to move to the match stage. Heather informed me that since the special needs portal wasn't functioning on the database, they requested Sofia's orphanage send the original referral paperwork and they would match me through CARA, India's adoption government agency, the traditional way prior to the database being established. Unfortunately, her orphanage was notorious for moving slowly. Heather anticipated it would be months before I would be formally matched. I fought discouragement daily. Heather assured me that since they were working directly with the orphanage, no other family would be able to match with Sofia. The orphanage would not permit it since they were the ones preparing her referral paperwork for me and the agency. Her proclamation was supposed to make me feel relieved, but seeds of fear had roots dug so deep in my heart, it seemed it would take years to fully extract them.

It was the beginning of February on a Thursday night as I sat down to obsessively check my email to begin my evening routine. I scrolled through my inbox and my heart stopped. An email from Heather caught my attention but it was the subject line that took my breath away: Pictures of Munni. I quickly opened the email.

Hi Kristen!
I just received the attached photos of Munni from the last visit to Hyderabad in January! Enjoy!

Attached were three of the most beautiful pictures I had ever seen. She was smiling. She had a dimple. She was missing one of her front teeth. I could not stop staring at the pictures. My heart felt like it was going to burst. These photos were everything the other pictures I had of her were not. They were the evidence of what I had been believing in my heart: buried deep within her was hope and joy and love. I couldn't contain my excitement. I immediately downloaded the pictures and sent an email to my mom. I sent an email to Mer, Sarah, Janet, and Kristen. I texted my sister the pictures. Giddy with joy, staring at her smiling face, I felt the fear subsiding in my heart. My Sofia. Anxiety loosened its grip and a shift began to take place. I still had no idea where the money would come from to pay for her adoption, but I knew she was my daughter, and I knew she was coming home.

I continued working and plodding through the paper chase. My social worker diligently corrected the edits for my home study to reflect what India wanted, while I simultaneously tracked down what seemed like a million documents for my dossier. I filled out several grant applications. The paperwork for the home study, dossier, and grants were more work than my thesis and Master's degree combined. I felt I deserved a Ph.D in adoption paperwork. For every required document, every medical exam, every notary, every blood draw, every fire inspection, for all of it, I tackled with tenacity, picturing her face the very first day I saw her. I had no control over India, but nothing was going to stop me from what I did have control over, and I made sure it was done as quickly as possible.

The middle of March, Heather called to tell me that Sofia's orphanage was sending four files of Hyderabad children, only her file wasn't one of them. Crushed didn't describe how I felt. Heather said it was actually a good thing they didn't send her file. Since the other agency had her file from last year, it was outdated. With the new system in place, India wanted all of the files to be in a distinct format. The way her Child Study Report and Medical Evaluation Report were filled out previously, the old format would cause a major delay at the point of when I would be waiting for my NOC, (No Objection Certificate), which allowed me to move forward to court. She assured me it was very fortunate that they caught it when they did because it forced them to update her CSR and MER to the new required format. Even though I was disappointed to be delayed a few weeks now, it was much better than facing this type of disappointment further down the line. I half-heartedly agreed with her.

With my home study completed and submitted for final review, the next set of fees were due. Thankfully, I had saved all of the money I earned from working at the pizzeria through January and February and paid those fees in full. However, since Sofia was a waiting child, the last set of fees would all be due at once. I couldn't even think about the pending amount because it made my stomach hurt. There was no way I could pay for it. The Lord would have to provide a miracle. Every day on my way to work, I prayed that God would part my Red Sea of finances. I prayed that He would rain down manna to bring Sofia home. The Mega Millions lottery grew larger than it ever had before, and I prayed like crazy that someone I knew would score a winning ticket. Crazy, I know. But I was desperate, and who was I to dictate how God would make this happen? If He could make bread fall from the sky to feed his people, He could certainly bless one of my friends with the golden ticket. It wasn't like I was playing the lottery myself. I also found out that I made it past the selection round for a grant organization. I didn't want to get my hopes up, but I prayed that if this was an avenue God was going to use, that He would continue to open the doors and allow me to progress to the next round.

To make matters more tense, my dad managed to continue his Inquisition every opportunity he had. Every time I drove to my parents' house for family dinner, I prayed God would give me strength, grace, and wisdom. My feelings were still crushed from December; instead of healing, the wound festered with infection from his constant jabs. My teenage rebellious mindset wanted nothing more than to prove him wrong. I begged God to show off, to shove it in my dad's face that Sofia was definitely coming home, that she was my daughter, and nothing was going to stop this from happening. I needed God to pull off the biggest miracle of my life. I printed a 5X7 copy of the picture of Sofia smiling with her missing front tooth, her sweet one dimple, and put magnetic tape on the back of it. I hung it on my parents' refrigerator in defiance. Whether he wanted to or not, my dad would see her face every day. I made sure of it. She was coming home and would be a part of this family. Every time he made his snide remark, "I don't know where you're going to get all that money," I took a deep breath and prayed. And every single time I answered him, "God will provide, Dad. You will see." But, it was a lot of money, and deep down, I wondered the same thing my dad questioned. I quoted scripture to myself to try and build my courage because doubt sat ready to pounce like a lion watching an injured gazelle. I left their house wringing my hands in prayer, begging God to please, please show up.

The beginning of April came, and the Mega Millions lottery reached the largest winning jackpot ever at $650 million. Three winning tickets sold, and for about five minutes, I held out hope that I knew one of the winners. Since that didn't pan out like I had hoped, I continued my search for other grant organizations, praying for a major miracle. At this point, I was working seven days a week. I had to pay for immigration and fingerprints. Although I knew I wouldn't have the full amount, I put every bit I could towards the looming final balance. Every time I started to get anxious about the money, I forced myself to read verses that I had scribbled down on index cards. I shoved them in my pants pockets, in my purse, in my jacket, in my car, in my server book at the restaurant. I said them out loud. I sang them in the shower. I said them in my car on my way to work. I prayed them incessantly. I was in constant dialogue with God about Sofia and money. I prayed for healing in her tender heart. I prayed for our relationship as mother and daughter. I prayed for the first moment when she saw me - that when I touched her, she would have an overwhelming feeling of love, safety, comfort, and joy. I prayed we would have supernatural bonding as mother and daughter. I prayed He would rain down financial blessings upon her adoption and that her fees would be paid in full. I prayed I would receive the grant from Gift of Adoption, the organization that contacted me in March to tell me I passed the first round. I prayed others would be blessed through helping us become a family. But most of all, I prayed for my dad's heart to be softened, so he would see that Sofia deserved to have a mom and a family who loved her. I prayed he would see that she was worth everything I was doing and more, that no amount of money could put a price tag on the value of her trading in the title of "orphan" for "daughter."

CHAPTER 16
DREAM - APRIL, 2012

I stood on the track, looking at my old high school football field. Only it wasn't a field. It was a giant swimming pool that spanned the entire space from goalpost to goalpost. The water was crystal blue and still like glass. On the other side of the pool stood the huge, wooden grandstands painted Kelly green. Giant oak trees towered behind them, and their branches gently swayed in the wind, creating a canopy of golden brown leaves on the warm, sunny day. At the very top row of the bleachers, to the left of the announcer's box, I could see Sofia sitting with an elderly couple. They appeared kind and had their arms around her. They were the only spectators to be seen. They looked down at me, and the elderly man waved.

As soon as I saw Sofia, an intense urge came over me to get to her as quickly as I could. Despite being dressed in a silk shirt and maxi skirt, I jumped right into the pool, fully clothed, and made my way to the other side. I climbed out, sopping wet with my clothes clinging to my body. I didn't care. I ran as fast as could, taking the steps two at a time until I reached the very top. I was desperate to get to her. I dropped to my knees, eye level to Sofia. I looked at her and scooped her up into my arms.

Instantly, we were standing in a doctor's office. It was white and sterile and the lights were almost blinding. The doctor was Indian and seemed pleasant. Sofia stood between us, chattering away in her dialect. What she was saying, I had no idea. The doctor was standing next to the examination table, holding his clipboard, and writing notes. Suddenly, he stopped, looked at her, and asked, "What is your name?"

"She doesn't speak English," I interjected.

Sofia stopped her chattering, looked at me, then turned to the doctor, and in perfect English stated, "My name is Munni."

"That's right!" I exclaimed, amazed at her English, "Your name is Sofia Munni!"

She shook her head no, and once again in perfect English declared, "My name is Munni."

I woke with a start. It took a minute to orient myself. I had held her in my arms. Another prayer answered. And with that answer, the last piece of my will that I had clung to in this adoption journey evaporated. It had been almost a year since finding Munni and reading her file. During that time, my spirit wrestled with changing her name. She had experienced tremendous loss in her life. Would losing her name add to her trauma? For almost twenty years, the name Sofia was synonymous with my daughter. I prayed about her name. Could I not have just this, I begged God? As the months passed, He slowly prepared my heart to hear His truth once more.

Tears rolled down my cheeks, and a smile spread across my face. My heart pulsated with joy and peace. I knew. He answered me. In that moment, I felt His incredible presence and total release of my will. No sadness, regret, or longing filled my heart. Instead, blessed assurance of what He knew all along:

My daughter's name is Munni Grae.

CHAPTER 17
REFERRAL

April 17, I received an email from Gift of Adoption that my grant application was tentatively scheduled for review at the May Grant Selection Committee meeting. My heart raced. Yesterday, Heather called me with the news that Munni's original referral paperwork was officially en route to the United States! She expected the paperwork to arrive in approximately two weeks! That put her referral arriving the first week of May. When I filled out the grant application, I took a bold step and asked for the full amount of $7500 dollars. It wasn't even half of the remaining balance, but if the committee approved me in May, it certainly would get me closer to paying it in full. I stared at the computer screen in disbelief of the timing. A smile spread across my face, and I silently thanked God and prayed that He would soften the committee's hearts toward my application. I asked Him to guide the committee to stamp 'approved' on my file.

I clicked on the link in the email. They wanted the most current updates to my application and had several questions for me to answer as I moved to the final round. The first few questions were a recap of my adoption journey. The third question left me with a sinking feeling. Have you signed an official referral for a child? I knew Munni's official paperwork was on the way, but I hadn't signed it. Semantics, I told myself as I typed "yes" in the box, knowing her referral would be signed in two weeks. As I moved on to the next question, my spirit stirred within me. I knew it was the Lord. I sat back in my chair and argued with God. I don't understand. This is a lot of money! Almost half! I'm signing those papers and by time this goes before the committee, it will be a true statement! The more I pleaded and tried to reason my case to God, the more convicted I became. I knew I had to change my answer to "no." I scrolled back to the question and positioned the mouse on the box. I wavered. Once again, I felt sick. I was on the edge of something great, only to watch it slip through my fingers. I breathed in, quickly typed "no." I hit submit before I lost what little faith and obedience I had. I leaned back in my chair and stared up at the ceiling. *You must have some magnificent miracle planned,* I silently prayed while fighting feelings of defeat.

Peace eventually flooded my heart for being truthful and changing my answer. As I reflected on the email and the request for updated information about my adoption, I decided that I would try to call the person in charge of the grants and explain my situation. The next morning, I woke with a sense of urgency. I needed to figure out a way to fast forward through the work day so I could make the phone call and plead my case. This was going to be longest eight hours. It seemed all I did in this adoption journey was wait, and I never improved in my ability to do it.

The school day finally ended. I raced out of the building and jumped into my car. I was anxious to get to my house and get this phone call started. I prayed the whole way home. I asked God to soften the lady's heart so she would be receptive to my situation. Most of all, I prayed my application would still be presented before the review committee. I let the dogs out so I wouldn't be distracted. I sat down on my sofa, took a deep breath, and dialed the numbers. The phone rang several times. With each ring, my heart seemed to beat louder.

"Ms. Gross, Grants manager," her answer sent my adrenaline into overdrive.

"Hello Ms. Gross! My name is Kristen Williams and my application is pending review. I wanted to call you because my situation is a little confusing, and I wanted to explain why I answered one of the questions the way I did when I received the email to update my status for the May review board," I tried to steady my voice, but it seemed like every word that came out of my mouth shook like a leaf in the wind.

"Okay, Ms. Williams. Give me a minute to pull up your application." I waited nervously for what seemed like an eternity.

"Here it is. This is for Munni's adoption?" she asked.

"Yes!"

"Can you tell me which question you were referring to?"

"Yes. It asked if I had signed an official referral. This is where my story is complicated. I found Munni on a waiting list June 16, 2011. I sent in my application and dossier to move forward with her adoption, but India suspended all adoptions before my dossier could be registered in India. It's been a journey of hurdles and waiting. Then, on November 14, the agency told me that because of the region where she is in India is very difficult to work with, they couldn't complete her adoption. I was devastated. However, a random lady found my blog and reached out to me. She is also trying to adopt a little girl from the same area of India, and she found a different agency who had an established relationship with the orphanage where Munni is. She spoke with them, and they assured her that they could facilitate the adoption. Sarah, that's the lady who found my blog, encouraged me to call the agency. I didn't waste any time. I called them, and they assured me that they could bring Munni home; in fact, my caseworker is adopting a little girl from the same orphanage, and Munni just happened to be in her daughter's referral picture," my words came tumbling out like toy blocks from a box.

"Oh my goodness!"

"I know. Well, during the suspension, India completely revamped their program and became party to the Hague Convention. All of these changes complicated how the paperwork would be handled with their new database they created. I'm registered online, but Munni is special needs, and the special needs portal isn't working. So, my agency requested that the orphanage send the original documents via mail. They were sent last week and are supposed to arrive in the United States at my agency next week. My agency will then overnight them to me so I can sign and have them notarized and apostilled. In regards to the update on the application for the grant, the question asked if I had signed the official referral. I very much wanted to type, "yes." I knew the referral was en route, but I didn't feel in good conscience I could say that I had signed official papers when in fact I hadn't. I called you because I wanted to explain my situation so that you knew where I was in my process. I'm so close!"

"Silence.

"Hello?" I asked.

"I'm shocked," Ms. Gross replied, "I really can't thank you enough for your honesty. Most people would have said, "yes." Your truthfulness goes a long way. I'll tell you what I'm going to do. I'm going to tell them everything you just told me," she declared, "and I'm going to recommend they award you the full amount."

"Oh my goodness." I could feel the tears coming. "I don't know what to say. Thank you so much!"

"Thank you for being honest. We need more of that. I appreciate you taking to the time to call and explain your situation."

"Thank you! I hope you have a wonderful day!" I exclaimed.

"Thanks. You too!"

I hung up the phone and screamed with excitement. I felt certain God convicted me to type, "no," so that He could bless me in this moment. I thanked Him and prayed the selection committee would heed Ms. Gross' recommendation. Receiving that grant would put a huge dent in the final fees. I smiled thinking how God was raining down my manna from heaven.

I continued working seven days a week, saving every penny, but it came at a cost. My stress levels were high, and my migraines were out of control. The next Friday night shift at the restaurant proved to be a disaster. Everything that could go wrong, did. Every rude customer found his way into my section. Customers left horrible tips, and everyone on my shift seemed to share my same bad mood. To top it off, it poured down rain and my closing sidework for the night was dealing with the sopping wet mats at the entranceway. It was the most dreaded sidework of all; those mats were disgusting to begin with, but when it rained, it was worse because they weighed a ton. Two times during the shift, I almost walked out. I had reached my breaking point. Instead, I stole away in the walk-in and reminded myself that for six and half years, I loved working there. It was an amazing company, and I didn't want my emotional state of mind to ruin that. I shoved shredded provolone cheese in my mouth while I prayed for the patience and mental strength to finish the shift.

It seemed it would never arrive but finally, I found the end of my shift. I turned in my server report, clocked out, and left. I had a feeling it was the last time I would walk out that back door. I walked to my car, got inside, and exhaled. *I can't do this anymore, God.* I continued to pour out my heart to Him. Ragged, weary, and worn out, I was completely spent. I cut my budget to the bare bones. I had been working seven days a week for months. I applied to every grant I could find. I did a few photography shoots to raise money. I found an online fundraising site called Ordinary Hero and asked people to purchase shirts, hoodies, hats, and jewelry on my behalf in hopes of winning a grant. The bonus of this company was that forty percent of the proceeds went towards Munni's adoption fees, whether or not I won the grant. Turned out, I didn't win the grant. Thankfully, my sister matched the grant anyway. In spite of all of these efforts, I hit a brick wall. The giant sum of money loomed over me like a tsunami; now was the worst time to quit my second job. But I had absolutely nothing left in me. I was completely burned out. I sent text messages to cover my Saturday and Sunday shifts. Maybe I'll feel better after taking a weekend off, I reasoned with myself as I turned the key in the ignition. Something deep in my spirit told me different.

I woke up the next morning, and I knew I couldn't go back. Stressed. Exhausted. Run down. However, I loved the people I worked with, and I did not want to leave on bad terms. I texted my manager and asked if we could talk. He texted me back and asked me to stop by the restaurant before it opened. I put on a baseball hat and headed out to my car. I prayed he would understand.

I walked in the door and saw Wes sitting in the back booth in the corner. My heart quickened its pace. This might be harder than what I anticipated, I thought to myself.

"Hey," Wes greeted me from the booth, "grab some coffee and come sit down."

I grabbed a cub of coffee and headed to the booth. I sat down and nervously smiled. I felt like a kid in trouble. I don't know why.

"What's going on?" Wes asked.

"I need a break," I replied.

"We can do that. No big deal," he responded, "Just put your shifts up like you're going on vacation and we can get them covered. Did you get tonight and tomorrow covered?"

"I did. But, here's the thing. I need a break, as in, longer than a vacation break." I could feel the tears building in the corners of my eyes. I loved working at the restaurant, and I loved the people I worked with. I loved my regulars. Making this decision, even though I knew it was the best thing for both my emotional and physical health, still hurt.

"Don't cry on me!" Wes panicked, "Honestly, Kristen, I've been waiting for this conversation for a long time. You've amazed me with how long you've been able to keep up with the schedule you've had. I don't know how you've done it. And on top of it, you always come in here with a positive attitude. Everyone loves working with you, and your customers love you. Take as much time as you need. If you want to come back in the summer when you're not teaching, and things are slower, you have a position waiting for you."

I wiped the tears from my eyes. "Thank you so much, Wes. This is really difficult because honestly, I like working here more than I like teaching. Isn't that unfortunate?" We both laughed.

"Hey," Wes looked right at me, "you do whatever you need to do to bring that beautiful daughter of yours home. Keep fighting. People see what you're doing. And it's amazing."

"Now you're really making me cry," I whimpered as I reached for a napkin to wipe my tears.

* * * * *

There were several families with my agency who were in my same position. We were all matched and being processed the traditional way while also being registered online through the new CARINGS database. Heather worked tirelessly to get us pushed through before the next cutoff. The goal was to send all of the families' dossiers in bulk by May 11. Munni's referral paperwork would make it just in time. If we didn't get through by May, that would push all of us back at least six months, where we would be stuck waiting for the special needs portal to be completed and for our children to be uploaded into the system. None of us wanted that to be our fate.

The last week of April, I finally completed my dossier and shipped it to my agency. I painfully discovered that when I had my documents notarized and sent off for the apostille, the state department sent them right back because they needed to be certified by the county clerk before the secretary of state would issue the apostille. I was not pleased. I had to drive to four different county clerks to certify all of the different notary signatures on my documents. One of the county clerks informed me that if I had any attorney friends, in the future it would save me the certification headache because it was not a requirement for attorney notarization since their notary never expires. Lesson learned. I filed away that valuable nugget of information, thinking about Munni's referral packet that would soon be on its way.

Late Wednesday afternoon, May 2, Heather sent me a quick email. Munni's documents had finally arrived. She explained that she would assemble all of the paperwork along with the instructions and then overnight them to me on Thursday. They should be on my doorstep by time I arrived home from school Friday afternoon. I needed to get them notarized, apostilled, and back to her by next Thursday, as all of the dossiers were being shipped in bulk on Friday, May 11. In addition, my account balance needed to be cleared and paid in full. It was crunch time!

I sent out texts asking for major prayers - first, that all of the money would be provided; and secondly, that I would be able to get all of the paperwork back to Heather in time. There was no way I would be able to get the apostilles completed and back in time through the mail. It was too risky, even with the overnight service. To complicate matters, my agency was on the west coast and I lived in the midwest. I couldn't take time off from school. Two critical pieces to this puzzle hung in the balance: I needed an attorney to notarize the papers, and I needed a courier.

I was about to be "that friend." I hadn't seen Danny in several years, but desperate times called for desperate measures. I decided our friendship of more than a decade could handle the awkward text. Besides, Danny was a great guy- funny, and always up for interesting situations. He was a real life Jerry Maguire who represented athletes and also taught classes for the University's Sport's Management program. I sat on my front porch and crafted my text:

"Hey Danny, it's Kristen! I think the last time we hung out was the Poison concert at Riverbend. lol! So, a lot has happened since then... I'm adopting a little girl from India! She's about to turn 6! This is the awkward part - I really need a huge favor from you. Sorry to be "that friend" Could you please, please, please, notarize some papers for me before Sunday? I will pay you! Or buy you beer. Or concert tix. It's an emergency and I can explain more in person. You would totally be doing me a solid. And I would be indebted to you forever. And ever."

I hit send and held my breath. I wasn't sure how he'd respond. He was pretty laid back, I hoped that would carry over into his reply. About an hour later, I heard my phone ding. I quickly checked my text messages. It was from Danny:

"Congrats on your little girl. Can you meet Friday down at UC before my 4 pm class? No need to pay me, glad to do it."

I couldn't believe it! All the pieces were coming together. With tears in my eyes, I quickly responded that I would gladly meet him at UC, and thanked him profusely. Now that the attorney piece was secured, I needed to line up my courier. I called my mom. Why did it seem like the phone rang forever every time I needed her to answer?

"Hi, Sweetie," her pleasant voice finally answered.

"MOM!" I yelled excitedly, "Guess what?"

"I don't know?"

"Munni's referral papers are at the agency and they will be on my door-step Friday afternoon when I get home from school!" I spilled with joy.

"Oh my goodness. That's amazing!" she responded.

"I still can't believe it. But, I need your help. Next week is going to be crazy."

"Why?" she asked.

"Well," I started to explain, "all of the dossiers are getting shipped next Friday. That means that I have to get all of Munni's referral papers signed, notarized, and the apostilles done and then all of those sent back to Oregon before next Thursday so Heather can double check that everything is in order. Then, everything gets shipped to India on Friday!"

"Kristen, it's like you are speaking in another language. Honestly, I'm amazed at all you have accomplished!"

"Thanks, Mom. I don't know if you remember the debacle I had with my dossier when I sent it to Columbus to get the apostilles, and they sent it back to me because I was missing the county certification?" I asked,

"Oh, that was terrible. And you had to drive around to all those different county offices getting signatures. You would think those people would come up with a better system," my mom started her rant.

"Mom, I texted Danny and he said he would meet me on Friday and notarize all of Munni's referral paperwork. Since he's an attorney, I don't have to do the county certification step."

"Oh! That is so nice of Danny."

"I know. He is saving my butt, seriously. Anyway, that will all be taken care of on Friday. I need a huge favor from you. I need you to drive up to Columbus on Monday, walk these documents through the secretary of state office for the apostilles, and then drop them off to me at my school. I have to make copies, and then I'll go immediately to the post office to overnight them to Heather. I want her to have two days to make sure she has absolutely everything she needs from me before the dossiers get shipped on Friday. I don't want anything to be missing from my end. Can you please do this for me?" I begged.

"Of course, I will," she assured me. "Just make sure you give me step-by-step instructions of what you need. Also, I need directions."

"I love you, Mom," I cried into the phone as emotion took over me. I still couldn't believe after all of the twists and turns I had been through, I was about to sign official papers accepting Munni as my daughter.

* * * * *

Friday finally arrived. I don't think my feet touched the ground the entire day; I floated through on pure joy and anticipation of arriving home to find Munni's referral documents waiting for me on my doorstep. When the final school bell rang, I raced out to my car and drove as fast as legally possible. Windows down, sun shining, radio on, I laughed the whole way home. It was literally one of the best days of my life! I couldn't wait to tear into the referral packet that I knew was waiting for me. I parked my car and ran up the steps to my front porch. Sure enough, waiting on my welcome mat was the most beautiful sight to behold: a Fedex package. I quickly bent down, picked it up, and opened my door. My dogs eagerly greeted me. They sensed the excitement and were ready to join in the party. I didn't have much time before I had to meet Danny. I carefully opened the packet and pulled out the most precious documents I've ever held in my entire life. I stared at them in disbelief. Heather had meticulously labeled each document with clear instructions of where and how to sign, and with what kind of pen. I quickly grabbed a sharpie for the photo signature and a blue ink pen for the rest. I let the dogs out and made sure I had everything I needed before quickly leaving again to meet Danny down on campus.

We had texted the night before and arranged a meeting spot. He only had a twenty minute window between classes and they were in two different buildings. By the grace of God, I found a parking spot on the main street in front of his second class. I texted him that I was in front of McMicken Hall in a white Xterra.

"On my way," he texted back.

My heart beat in eager anticipation. I was about to sign the most important papers of my life! I couldn't stop smiling. I looked out the passenger window up the hill and saw Danny walking towards my car. I got out quickly, ran around my car, and onto the sidewalk. "Hey!" I cheerily reached out to hug him, "It's been awhile! Thanks so much for doing this!"

"No problem. So, you've been busy!" Danny replied.

"I know! I'm so excited! I can tell you about it while we sign papers. How do you want to do this?"

"We can just do it in your car. My briefcase is a hard case, so you can sign on it," Danny suggested.

"I feel like we're doing a street deal," I laughed as we both got back into the car.

"Hey, that's how we roll!"

I showed Danny all of the paperwork and exactly how each paper had to be signed and notarized. He did a few practice stamps to make sure it was right side up and we were ready to go. I started with the first paper and began to write out the sentence exactly how Heather had instructed me to write on each document:

I accept Munni as my daughter May 4, 2012

I finished writing and stared at the paper. It was the most beautiful sentence I had ever written. The lump in my throat grew to the point I couldn't speak. I looked up at Danny and all emotion came tumbling out in tears.

"Aw, do you need a hug?" Danny asked.

Still unable to speak, I nodded my head and leaned in for his embrace. I cried into his shoulder. I couldn't believe I actually wrote those words! After a moment, I pulled back and got myself together. "Thank you. That sentence really hit me. This journey has been unbelievably hard. There have been so many twists and turns, stops, dead ends. Times when I thought I completely lost her. It's been incredibly painful, and I almost gave up because I lost hope. But, God has been faithful to me. He continued to push me and give me glimmers of hope, some of them were barely a flicker, but they were there. So, I kept pursuing her. One thing would lead to another way opening, or a random encounter would end up opening a door. It was crazy, Danny. So when I wrote that sentence," my voice cracked, "I realized how nothing is too hard for God. Back in December, when I was at my lowest point, He brought that verse to me, how nothing is too hard for the Lord ;[4] and look what I'm doing right now!" I finished through my trembling, crying voice. "I'm just completely blown away!"

"It's pretty amazing!" Danny agreed.

Fifteen minutes later, we finished signing and stamping all of the paperwork. I gave Danny a high five. "I will never be able to thank you enough for this. I can't put a price tag on it. Can I attempt to show you my gratitude through concert tickets? Beer? Dinner? Anything?"

"Yes. Introduce me to your daughter when she gets home," Danny said as he got out of my car.

"You're a good friend, Danny."

"Take care, and I hope the rest of your process goes quickly!" Danny said as he shut the door and turned to walk back up the hill.

I sat in my car completely humbled and thankful. Still in disbelief I had signed her referral papers, I looked at the huge stack of documents on the passenger seat. I stared at Munni's picture with my signature scribbled across her face. My daughter. Joy filled my heart as I turned on my car and headed home.

*   *   *   *   *

Sunday night arrived, and I drove to my parent's house for dinner. I prepared my documents for my mom's courier service she was providing me the next day so I could overnight my dossier to Heather. I dreaded another interrogation from my dad about the hefty fees that weighed over me, but I was determined to stay positive and focus on all the forward progress that had been made.

Lively political discussions during dinner secured my escape from any potential questioning from my dad. Too busy debating with my sister, my dad focused on antagonizing her. I narrowly dodged a heated grill session. I continued my silent prayers for a smooth, positive evening. I decided to wait until my sister's family left before I brought up my mom's trip to Columbus the next day. I figured that would only invite meddling from my dad and certain persecution. I hoped he would go to bed and I could avoid it altogether.

God answered my prayers as my dad retired to his bedroom as soon as my sister and her family left. My mom and I looked at each other with relief and quickly got to planning her trip. I explained each document, gave her the check for the apostille fee along with the cover sheet, and written out directions just in case. The only snag in all of this was a huge storm system was forecasted to move through the area right as my mom would be making the two hour trek. My mom hated driving in the rain; it made her nervous. I knew this was a true act of love on her behalf. I sent out a prayer chain asking for protection for my mom and for a smooth, quick turnaround.

The next morning, I woke to rumbling thunder. I immediately prayed for my mom. The butterflies started fluttering and continued all day. Despite an activity-filled teaching schedule, I couldn't help but wonder where my mom was in the process. Did she find the building without any problem? Did everything go smoothly? Was she back on the road? Finally, at 1:20 p.m., my classroom phone rang. I quickly picked it up.

"Hi, Kristen," Donna, the school secretary said in her sweet voice. "Your mom is here with some very important papers."

"Oh my goodness. I'll be right out!" I squealed as I quickly hung up the phone.

My classroom was conveniently positioned right outside the office. I opened the door to see my mom standing there, a stack of papers in hand, and a huge smile spread across her face. I ran up to her and gave her a giant hug. "I love you, Mom! Thank you so much!" I told her as I felt the tears coming. Overwhelmed by all the pieces coming together, I silently thanked God for protecting my mom and getting her back safely. "How did everything go? Did you hit any storms on the way up?"

"Not a single rain drop! I did have a little trouble finding the building. They moved their office, so the address you gave me wasn't the current one."

"Oh no!" I replied, feeling awful for the mixup. "Was it far from the original location?"

"No, only a few blocks. And everyone was very kind and helpful," my mom reassured me.

"Did Dad say anything?" I nervously inquired.

"He grumbled about the drive. But then he said something along the lines of, 'so this is really happening'," my mom said with a sly smile.

I looked at her. "It's about time he's figuring it out. She's coming home!" I quickly hugged her goodbye and turned around to go back to my classroom. I was greeted by a roomful of eager students staring at me with excited faces.

One student spoke up, "Señorita, is that for your adoption?"

"Yes! It's a major step forward!" I answered excitedly. Months earlier, I had told my students about my adoption, and they eagerly cheered me on.

Another student asked, "Was that your mom? You look just like her!"

"It was! And she's amazing because she just pulled off the biggest miracle I needed in order to get my dossier to India by Friday!"

"Well, that's what moms are for," the student answered matter-of-fact.

He had no idea the weight of the truth he spoke in that simple sentence. I felt a tightening in my throat, thankful for my mom and her willingness to act not only for me, but for my daughter as well. Her self-sacrifice today set in motion all of the things that needed to happen that would allow my dossier to be shipped to India on Friday. I thought about the future and what it held for Munni and me. I couldn't wait for the opportunities to come to her rescue the way my mom came to mine.

CHAPTER 18
MOVING MOUNTAINS

My new Friday night routine consisted of obsessively checking my gmail. Instead of refilling drinks, I searched for emails from Gift of Adoption in hopes they awarded me the grant. I mindlessly scrolled through my email when a new one from Heather popped up in my inbox. The subject made my heart skip a beat: Documents are on their way to India!

I quickly opened the email. She sent all of our dossiers to India. I kept reading - She didn't want to risk any of our dossiers being delayed, so she sent them trusting that we will pay our balances in full on Monday. Monday. My throat tightened and my skin started to itch. I tried not to panic, but my heart began to race. Fear stood outside, banging on the door of my heart, trying its hardest to barge its way in. My faith huddled in the corner like a small child clutching her teddybear, hoping against hope her dad would come to her rescue. If ever I needed God to show up in my life, it was now. I needed a miracle. A giant, part-the-Red-Sea, miracle. My phone rang and snapped me out of beseeching God for His divine intervention. It was Wiggins.

"Hey friend! Just calling to check in and see how things are going."

"Hey. I'm freaking out," I admitted.

"What? Why?"

"Money."

"How close are you to being fully funded?" she asked.

My stomach instantly twisted, my body was in full panic mode. "Um, I'm nowhere near being fully funded. I keep praying for the Gift of Adoption grant. I've checked my email relentlessly, hoping for an update. Kristen,

I'm stressing big time about the money," I confessed, "and I just got an email from Heather that our accounts have to be paid in full by Monday."

"How much do you need?" she inquired.

I took a deep breath. I had yet to say the number out loud. "The final fee is $18,050.00," my statement hung in the air and the impossibility of it swirled in my head to epic proportions.

"That's nothing for God. Look at everything He's done so far. Also, don't forget about the verse He gave you in December. It's a touchstone for times like these. He's going to see you all the way through until she is home!"

"Ugh! This trusting stuff is so hard and scary!" I lamented, "I literally have no idea where this money is going to come from. Even if I get the grant, it still won't cover everything. I have $3,300 saved from Dewey's and then $409 from Ordinary Hero fundraising that they are going to transfer. So whatever that equals is what I owe."

"I think you should put it on your blog," Kristen suggested.

"You do?"

"Absolutely. People don't know. And I think you should be transparent about everything you've done. How much you've paid, what you've fundraised, and what you still need. From that point on, let God work. You never know whose heart He will soften or whose heart has been touched by your story."

"It's humbling to ask for money," I admitted.

"It is," she agreed, "but you're also allowing others the opportunity to be a part of this beautiful story! Besides, specific prayer is critical, and by putting your specific amount needed on your blog and asking for prayer in regards to that will be powerful. You have so many people praying for you and sweet Munni!" she encouraged me.

"Okay, you've convinced me! I'll sacrifice my pride and humble myself. Anyway, you're right. It's not about me. It's about God and His glory because there's no way I can pull this off. It's going to be all Him. It's just weird when it comes to money. I hate that."

"That's why it's usually one of the biggest tools He uses to refine people. I'm excited to watch this all unfold! I'm praying for you, Williams!"

"Thanks. Love you and love all your encouragement."

"Love you, too."

I hung up the phone and heeded Kristen's advice. I wrote a blog post detailing the financial mountain that stood in the way of my dossier being submitted and asked for specific prayer. God had one weekend to move this mountain. I needed all the prayer I could get. I couldn't sit around so I put the leashes on my dogs and headed out for a long walk. I prayed for strength and faith to get me through this trial. I prayed for the hearts of those who would read my blog post. I meditated on two verses as I walked. I thought about the verse in John. Jesus said, "If you ask me anything in my name, I will do it."[5] I thought about the verse from James regarding pure and genuine religion and caring for the orphan.[6] What I was asking from God was according to his will. What better way to care for the orphan than to provide a family? I prayed He would be glorified and hearts would be softened. I prayed He would remove the fear from my heart. I knew fear wasn't from Him; it was a battle that still needed to be conquered.

The sun was setting, so we headed back to the house. As we came up the stone path, I slowly walked through my garden. I paused at my favorite flowers, Angel Cheeks peonies. I watched as the tiny ants crawled all over the huge, swollen buds. I knew in a week or so, those buds would reveal petals upon petals of the most beautiful, showy blooms in my entire garden. They were my show stoppers. The ants fascinated me how they worked. Busily marching deep into the bud to retrieve the nectar, their ordered pathways would be the catalyst that break open the magnificent bloom. I watched for few more minutes when I got a tingling sensation. My heart quickened as I looked at those tiny ants on that gorgeous flower still hidden in its bud. Who would have imagined that the tiniest of insects played such a pivotal role in the bloom of one of the most exquisite spring flowers? Standing in my garden, I felt in my spirit that God used those ants to calm my fears. His thoughts and His ways were not my thoughts and my ways; they were so much higher, more than I could ever imagine.[7] If He created and ordered ants to be part of the blooming process of peonies, surely He had a plan to move this financial mountain. I wondered where my ants were and when they would show up. I turned and walked up the steps and into my house.

I fed the dogs and checked my email again. Nothing from Gift of Adoption. Ugh. I fought back the panic rising in my chest. Instead, I clicked on Facebook for a distraction. There was a message in my inbox. I clicked on it. It was from my best friend from high school. She's never on Facebook. I quickly opened it.

Hey there! I just checked your blog which looks like you just updated it today. I have news for you. Although it's not the $14,000 that you need - I will drop a check off at your sister's house tomorrow (Sat) for $500 ;) I have wanted to help and contribute to your fight to get your little ones since you started the blog and I haven't. If you hadn't seen in the news/papers the beginning of April - I along with a few coworkers won a little money in the lottery when it hit the big ticket. Not life changing - but I can't think of a better way to help make three people's lives life changing. Consider it a Mother's Day present. You will be an awesome mom very soon. You already are. Love and miss you - Jenny

Tears poured down my face. I started sobbing. Minutes ago, I was standing in my garden staring at ants wondering how God was going to move this mountain. Not only did He provide, but He answered a prayer I had prayed months ago. I specifically prayed for someone I know to win the lottery. I was blown away! What in the world?! I almost couldn't take it all in, I was completely overwhelmed by the magnitude of His love. I thanked Him for Jenny. I thanked Him for blessing her. I prayed that He would bless her for blessing me. I prayed that He would continue to soften hearts and move the rest of the mountain. Sunday was Mother's Day. Wouldn't it be amazing if all the money came together by then? I timidly prayed for a Mother's Day miracle.

*   *   *   *   *

Mother's Day arrived and with it so did several checks in the mail. The timing was crazy as they were all stamped before I had posted my blog. On Saturday, two friends swung by and dropped off donations. Everyone cheered me on and prayed for the rest of the money to come in. Completely humbled and thankful, I spent my entire weekend in tears.

I arrived at my grandma's house for our annual Mother's Day celebration. I had mixed emotions. I was excited and also nervous. I still battled the fear of facing my dad's never-ending Inquisition. Despite all of the generosity that had been poured out upon my adoption, I still needed $13,160 to clear my balance. I checked my email constantly, but no updates from Gift of Adoption awaited me.

I walked to the backyard, where all the festivities took place, and greeted everyone. My sister gave me a hug and slipped me the check from Jenny.

"How much do you still need?" she asked.

"A lot. I'm trying not to be nervous. I need $13,160."

"We're praying for you. That's a big check Jenny gave you!" my sister said surprised.

"Do you know the story?" I asked her.

"No, tell me."

I rewound to March, when I first prayed about the lottery, and how I specifically prayed that God would bless someone I know. I told her the whole story, the timing of her message in regards to my blog post, how Jenny's never on Facebook, everything.

"Wow! That's incredible," my sister replied.

"I know. I'm amazed. But today, you just have to help keep me away from Dad. He's going to start asking about how much I owe and you know how he gets. I don't want to get into it with him. Especially after our big blowout last December."

"Don't worry. He never stays long at these things anyway," my sister laughed. "He's probably going to go play golf or go home and take a nap."

"For real. Let's hope!" We both laughed.

The rest of the afternoon went smoothly for the most part, except my dad never left early. Instead, he followed me to my car as I was getting ready to leave.

"When do you need to pay all of your fees?" he started his interrogation.

"Tomorrow night. My agency is on the west coast," I tried to answer confidently.

"Do you have all of the money?" His eyes pierced mine as he asked.

"Not yet. But, I will. God is faithful, Dad. Munni is coming home. You'll see," I said as I got into my car and started to shut the door.

"Okay. If you say so," he replied.

I put on my seatbelt, waved goodbye, and drove off. I managed to hold back the tears until I was out of sight. I begged God to please, please provide the money. I had no tricks up my sleeve. No hidden money under my mattress. No long, lost valuables to sell. Nothing. I had nothing. It was entirely in God's hands. And I was terrified.

*   *   *   *   *

I barely slept. I woke at 2 a.m. with a giant migraine. I knew the stress was taking its toll. I took my medicine and tried to go back to sleep. It seemed only five minutes had passed when my alarm buzzed that it was time to wake up. Exhausted, I got out of bed. At least my migraine was gone. I stood in the hot shower and prayed for a miracle. I had the whole day ahead of me; events awaited, of which I had no idea how they would unfold. However it was going to happen, I continued to beg God to move the mountain. The thought of being delayed at least another six months made me sick to my stomach. I couldn't even think about it.

I checked my email throughout the day only to be met with disappointment. Panic had set in, and I felt desperate. I didn't understand. Based on my conversation with Ms. Gross at Gift of Adoption, I thought for sure my application would have been presented before the May committee. It didn't make sense that I didn't hear anything from them. I decided I would call her after school and explain my situation. Things were dire, and I needed to capitalize on any and all resources I had.

I didn't even wait to get home. I called her from my car. Discouragement hit me once again; her voicemail greeted me. In a frenzied tone, I left a detailed voicemail explaining my situation. I left my phone number, my email, and my agency information. I covered all the bases. I prayed God would move her heart to plead my case to the committee. I prayed the committee would move to approve my grant request. There was nothing else I could do. I drove home in frustration; I wanted to come out of my skin. I hated waiting. I hated trusting. I hated not knowing how any of this was going to turn out. I hated that Munni sat in an orphanage not knowing that I was fighting for her with everything that I had. I needed God to show up. He had to provide a miracle. I needed Him to completely destroy that mountain.

Being at home with nothing to do was worse; it only fueled my obsessive email checking habit. I felt like a caged animal just sitting at my house, so I put the leashes on my dogs. We got in my car and headed to the park. I needed fresh air, sunshine, and a long walk. We hit the dog park after our walk, and they burned off some extra energy. It was a good distraction. Finally, we got back in the car to head home. I checked my phone. No missed calls. I checked my email. None. What in the world was God doing? I exhaled and stared at the tree line. I hadn't eaten all day because of my nerves, and my stomach finally started to growl. I turned on my car and started to head home. Right as I was about to pull out of the park, my phone rang. I quickly picked it up and looked at the caller ID: Mom and Dad home. Disappointed that it wasn't Gift of Adoption, I reluctantly answered the phone,

"Hey, Mom."

"Don't sound so excited," my dad's voice caught me by surprise. Great. This was not what I needed. I could not handle a grill session from him right now.

"Oh hey, Dad. I thought it was Mom."

"What are you doing?" he asked.

"I'm just driving back from the park with the dogs," I tried to sound casual.

"Oh. Well, did you get all the money?" he didn't waste any time asking the big question.

I took a deep breath. "No. Not yet," I answered, somewhat deflated.

"How much do you need?" he continued his inquiry.

"A lot."

"How much?"

"Dad, a lot," I answered annoyed.

"Kristen, how much?" his irritation was growing.

Another deep breath. "$13,160," I responded. I waited for his onslaught.

"Don't you need that by tonight?"

"Yes."

"Well, come to the house. I have a check waiting for you," he replied.

So many thoughts swirled in my head. "Dad, you don't have to do this."

"Kristen, I wouldn't do it if I didn't want to. Now, come to the house and get the check," he said.

"Okay," I responded in a cracked voice.

"And bring the dogs," my dad added.

Twenty minutes later, I arrived at my parent's house. I didn't know what to think. In December, my dad didn't want to give me $4000 to start her adoption. Now he was about to hand me a check for three times that amount. It didn't make any sense. I got out of my car and grabbed the dogs' leashes and walked into the house.

"I hear puppy dogs!" my dad yelled from the T.V. room. My dogs followed his voice excitedly.

"Hey!" I responded.

My mom came in the kitchen and gave me a hug. "Hi, Sweetie."

"Hi, Mom. What's going on with Dad?" I asked in a quiet voice.

"It was his idea, Kristen. He wanted to do it," my mom answered me. We both looked at each other in disbelief.

"God has really softened your dad's heart," my mom quickly ended her sentence as my dad came into the kitchen.

"Hi, Kris," my dad greeted me.

"Hey, Dad. How are you?"

"Good. How are you?" he asked, smiling like he did on Christmas morning when he was about to give a big gift.

"Nervous," I admitted.

He laughed. "Well, wait a minute." He turned and walked to the shelf where he kept his wallet and keys. He picked up a check and walked back into the kitchen. He looked at me and handed me the check. "This is for you and your daughter," he declared.

I took the check and looked at it. I've always loved my dad's handwriting. I stared at what he wrote. Pay to: *Kristen Grae Williams*. He wrote the check for the full amount. He signed it with his usual signature, *Richard Grae Williams*. And then, I looked at the memo. Written in his beautiful handwriting, he made a bold declaration. On that memo line, three beautiful words:

Munni Grae Williams.

Our namesake. His affirmation was not lost on me. Blinded by tears, all I could do was nod my head as I leaned in and hugged my dad.

He kissed the top of my head, "I love you."

"I love you, too," I cried.

Not one for staying in a sentimental moment, my dad quickly reprimanded me, "You better deposit that in the ATM tonight so it can start the clearing process. Are you going to let your agency know that you have the money?"

I wiped my tears and recomposed myself. "I'm going to send Heather an email right now to let her know," I reassured him.

"Okay. Did you already eat dinner?"

"No. I haven't eaten all day. My nerves were shot."

"Why don't you stay for dinner?" he offered.

"Thanks, Dad. I will."

"Why don't we all have a glass of wine?" he suggested.

"That sounds terrific!" my mom answered.

"Fill mine all the way to the top," I joked.

"Right!" my dad laughed.

I sat down at the kitchen table and sent a quick email to Heather explaining the situation. I had the money but it would be a day or two before the check cleared my account. Then, I logged into my blog and wrote a quick post: Mountain moved. Balance paid in full. Then, I shared it on social media. I took a sip of wine and thanked God for the incredible miracle He performed. Not only in providing the money, but in changing my dad's heart. He transformed my dad's attitude and restored our relationship. No wonder I never heard from Gift of Adoption. God had something far greater in mind, something I never would have dreamed or imagined.

CHAPTER 19
SUMMER 2012

The end of June crept up on me as I had kept busy with immigration errands and early summer gardening. The immigration process had moved smoothly. Mer gave me a tip to bypass waiting for my fingerprint appointment and instead, told me to just show up with my appointment letter and beg the officer to print me on the spot. I followed her advice. I drove down to the federal building. Once inside, I pleaded, showed Munni's picture, and shared my story. It worked like a charm. The officer took me back and processed my fingerprints immediately. That tip sped up my process by three weeks. Two major approvals quickly followed, which just left Article 5 - the last immigration piece that stated I did everything on the U.S. side according to the Hague Convention

The grant had somewhat slipped my mind since my dad paid the remaining balance of my final fees, which is why it caught me by surprise when I received an email from Gift of Adoption requesting an application update. The email informed me that my application was up for review before the combined June/July committee. This email was more involved than the previous email I had received; it requested an essay of my adoption journey to date. I sat down, and for the next two hours, I spilled my heart out as I crafted a composition detailing the incredible journey that led me to my daughter. I shared the twists, turns, and seemingly closed doors I encountered along the way. But through it all, I never gave up because I knew she was my daughter. I read and reread it. How do you express in an essay everything this journey has been? It was impossible. I had to trust that the words I wrote were enough. Finally, I hit send. I prayed it touched the hearts of those who made the final decision. Heather made it clear several weeks prior that I would definitely have to make two trips to Hyderabad - one for court and a second for pick up. This new revelation dramatically increased the amount of money I still needed to bring Munni home. Winning this grant would be a huge relief.

Two weeks passed. On July 10, I checked my email to find the grant selection committee approved my application. Included in the email was a link with the details of the approved amount and information about the grant disbursement. It felt like Christmas morning. I anxiously clicked the link to find the award that awaited me:

> The Gift of Adoption Fund has awarded, Kristen Williams ("Recipients") a grant of up to $7,500.00 to assist with fees directly related to completing Recipients' adoption.

I gasped! I read it again. Stunned, I pushed my chair back and held my hands over my mouth. Tears running down my face, I thanked God for yet another miracle. They gifted me the full amount. I thought back to May and the final fees due for Munni's adoption. In my mind, I needed the grant to be approved to help me get a majority of those funds covered. Once again, God showed me how His ways are so much higher than my ways. He had been softening my dad's heart and working on a restoring our relationship, and He did it in a way more beautiful and more powerful and more meaningful than anything I ever could have imagined. There wasn't a doubt in my mind that He caused the grant committee to put my application on hold. Now that I knew two trips to Hyderabad were required, winning this grant, for this amount, came at the perfect time. I laughed through my tears at the wonder of God's love for me, for Munni, and His incredible ability to orchestrate every single detail to perfection.

The following week, I finally received the email from the U.S. Embassy in New Delhi. They issued my Article 5 clearance. I jumped up and down in excitement. My dogs joined in the celebration, eager to share in my joy. I emailed Heather and attached the Article 5 letter. I asked her about the timing of India's NOC (No Objection Certificate), which would allow my case to move to the court process. I was completely in shock that things were moving as quickly as they were. Every single day, I prayed fervently over

Munni, over our relationship, over the paperwork, over the process. I prayed like it was my full time job. I felt certain God was honoring my prayers. I skipped through the next several hours filled with joy.

I came in from gardening and checked my email. Heather responded and congratulated me on receiving Article 5. Her next sentence took all the wind out of my happy sails. She told me that NOC can take up to six months, and she reminded me that India is the land of tomorrow. She urged me to put NOC on the back burner otherwise, I would drive myself crazy. She said for her personal case, it took three months to get NOC. Since her daughter was in the same orphanage as Munni, I used her timeline as a gauge. By time I finished reading her email, I felt all of the jubilation sucked out of me. Three months was a long time. I didn't even allow myself to think about six months. I tried not to mentally calculate, but I couldn't help it. If I didn't get NOC until October or November, then I wouldn't be in court until sometime in the next year. And Heather said it was a good two months between the trips so that meant I wouldn't bring Munni home until next summer. My heart sank. I fought to keep my thoughts positive, but the rest of the day was an enormous mental battle. Sadness once again infiltrated my spirit and took up residence. I hated thinking about Munni living in an orphanage day in and day out. All I wanted to do was get over there and bring her home with me. I texted several friends and asked them to pray for me. I told them about the situation and asked for encouragement and perseverance through this next long waiting stretch.

The next morning, I woke up with the weight of sadness on my chest. I hated feeling this way. I knew I needed to stay busy. I got up and made a schedule for my day. Once school started again, that would help with the distraction, but these long summer days could be potentially mentally and emotionally damaging if I didn't plan accordingly. I didn't want to slip into a horrible, sad place.

I managed to make it through the morning with a great prayer time and long walk with the dogs. I moved on to gardening and was quite pleased with how my flowers were looking. I dead-headed blooms, pulled weeds, and cleaned up the grounds. Before I knew it, I had filled four large garden bags. I went inside to take a water break. I stood at my sink filling my water bottle and looked out my window into my backyard. I noticed my hummingbird feeder was empty. I took a gulp of water and then walked into the back yard to get the hummingbird feeder. I brought it in the kitchen and rinsed it out. My mom taught me how to make my own hummingbird food, so I got out my saucepan, sugar, and measuring cup. I portioned out the sugar and water, put everything in the saucepan, and put it on the burner to melt the sugar into the water. The hummingbirds loved this sugar water recipe! I rinsed my sticky fingers when I heard my phone ring. I quickly dried my hands and ran to my phone. It was Heather. I answered before it stopped ringing, "Hey, Heather!"

"Hi, How are you?" she replied.

"I'm okay. Trying to enjoy the last of my summer break," I laughed, trying to sound casual.

"Are you sitting down?" she asked.

"No. Do I need to?" I started to worry.

"I think you should," she responded.

"Oh gosh," I said as I walked out to my front porch and sat down in the chair. "Okay, I'm sitting down. I'm nervous," I confessed.

"Well, nervous is not the emotion you should be," Heather stated. "Excited or bewildered are better ones. Congratulations! You got your NOC."

"What?" I sat in a daze. I could not process what I thought she had said.

"You got your NOC!" she repeated with greater enthusiasm.

Her words sank in and the reality of it hit me. "OH MY GOODNESS!" I screamed! My heartbeat accelerated and I jumped up from the seat. "When? I can't believe this. I thought it was supposed to take three to six months? Yesterday, I was so sad and today, I woke up feeling completely depressed. HEATHER!"

"I know. Quite frankly, we are all shocked," Heather informed me. "We have never seen this happen. Ever."

"I can't even process this!" I said excitedly.

WOOOOOOOOP WOOOOOOOP WOOOOOOOOP WOOOOOOOOP My fire alarm shrieked, shocking me back to reality. Oh no! I forgot about the sugar water on the stove.

"What is that noise?" Heather inquired.

"Uh, well, I was," I quickly opened my front door and was greeted with a cloud of smoke. I ran to my kitchen and grabbed the pan off of the stove, quickly putting it in the sink. I doused cold water over the charred, encrusted, sugar.

"Kristen, are you okay?" Heather asked.

I tried to undo the battery from the fire alarm as fast as I could. "Yeah, um, right before you called," the stupid fire alarm kept shrieking, "I was boiling sugar water for the hummingbirds." I finally got the battery out of the fire alarm. "When the phone rang, I answered it, and it was you, and then you told me the fantastic news, and I was on the front porch and forgot all about the water on the stove until the alarm, but I promise I'm really responsible in the normal day-to-day life stuff!" I rambled to her.

"I'm sure you are," she laughed. "Well, at this point in the process, you will switch over to Lisa. She handles everything on the India side. She will call you in the next day or two. However, since our girls are in the same orphanage, I would love to stay in touch if that's alright with you?"

"Oh my goodness, I would love that!" I responded.

"One more thing. Since you have NOC, you can now start working on a photo book to send to Munni. You should include photos of your house, inside and out. Photos of you, your family, anything or anyone that she will encounter on a daily basis. When you have it finished, send it in and depending on my court affidavit, either I will be able to hand deliver it to her, or we will courier it to India."

"This made my whole summer!" I exclaimed, "Seriously, I am so happy and excited and overwhelmed in the best way! I can't believe you will be traveling for court soon! This is all so amazing!"

"That's the thing about India," Heather mused. "It's like you wait and wait and wait and then all of a sudden, everything moves. There's no predicting it; it just happens. Without warning."

"No kidding! I think I'm still in shock!"

"Well, go celebrate this exciting news. You've just cleared a HUGE hurdle!" Heather exclaimed.

"Thank you! I'm going to call everyone I know. GAH! I'm so excited I don't know what to do with myself. Thank you so much, Heather. I hope you have an awesome day, and I will get to work on the book and send it to you soon."

"Sounds great. Take care."

I hung up the phone, turned to Simon, grabbled him by the ears, and gave him a big kiss right between his eyes. He wagged his nub. I laughed. I couldn't believe it! Just yesterday, she told me that I should expect to wait months for this approval. Never would I have suspected a phone call from her today receiving this unbelievable update. Still stunned, I started calling everyone in my inner circle. I was eager to share this miraculous news. With each phone call I made, my excitement waned as no one answered their phone. Frustrated that I couldn't share my good news, I decided to run a few errands to kill some time until someone called me back.

Just as I left the jewelry store from picking up my ring, my good friend Jennifer called me back. "What's going on?" she asked as soon as I answered.

"I GOT NOC!" I screamed into the phone.

"No way!"

"YES!" I affirmed.

"Come over!" she told me. "We need to celebrate."

"I'm on my way."

I hung up the phone, all of my joy and excitement rushed back full force. What a summer it had been. Ten minutes later, I pulled into her driveway. I walked up to her front porch, and Murphy, her dog, greeted me with his signature howl. I opened her screen door and walked into her living room. Jen came out from her kitchen and around the corner. We looked at each other with tears in our eyes. I took two steps toward her and fell into her arms sobbing. Almost ten years prior, we had met through a small group at our church. We were both single and instantly formed a friendship over a similar sorrow. We both desired marriage and family, however; those dreams eluded us for longer than the normal societal standards. We each bought our houses as singles, we were both teachers, and we spent many nights drinking wine, lamenting with one another, and praying for each other. For years, we lived the single life, encouraging each other as we plodded on, day after day, month after month, year after year. Jen eventually met her husband. Later, they were blessed with twins. When I told her I was adopting, she walked right beside me, encouraging and praying for me. She kept a picture of Munni on her refrigerator, praying for her daily.

I managed to get my emotions under control. I pulled back and looked at Jen. "Can you believe it? I have my NOC!"

"I am shocked!" she stated. "But even more excited to celebrate," she laughed as she grabbed a bottle of red wine and the bottle opener.

I laughed. "I can't think of a better reason to drink wine at two in the afternoon."

"I can't either." she agreed.

As I watched Jen poured two glasses of red wine, my mind swirled with wonder at all that God had done. Something in my conscious gnawed at me with fear. I did not feel good about where she was, and I prayed for her protection. I desperately wanted her home. For some reason, I sensed an urgency to get her out of there. Thinking about how quickly things had moved this summer, especially in her region, which was notorious for being extremely difficult, I couldn't help but praise God for the miracles He continued to perform.

Jen handed me a glass. "To your daughter, Munni!"

I lifted my glass. "To Munni!"

* * * * *

The next day, my phone rang. It was my agency. I eagerly answered the phone. "Hello?"

"Hi, am I speaking with Kristen?" a kind voice replied on the other line.

"This is she," I responded.

"Hi, Kristen. This is Lisa. I have to tell you, I am so happy to finally get to talk to you! Munni is a precious, precious little girl. I have tried to find her a family for years, and when Heather told me about you last December, I thanked God for answering my prayers for her."

"Oh my goodness, Lisa!" I exclaimed. I couldn't believe what she was telling me. "Wait, well, first, hi! But, you know Munni? Have you met her? I have so many questions!"

"I have," Lisa answered, "I've seen her every time I went to Hyderabad. She is one that has weighed heavy on my heart."

I could feel all of my emotions rise to the surface. I felt an instant connection with Lisa - I don't know if it was her heart for Munni, the kindness in her voice when she talked about her, or the sense I got from her that I could tell she truly cared for Munni. Whatever it was, I felt she was an immediate kindred spirit. I spent the next two hours pouring out my heart to Lisa. I recounted my adoption journey, describing all of the miracles that had taken place. I expressed my deep love and devotion for Munni. I was sobbing by time I finished. Lisa, moved by all I shared with her, also cried.

"I have to tell you, one time in particular that I went to Hyderabad, I couldn't even take pictures of Munni because she looked so bad. She was covered head to toe in huge boils. It absolutely broke my heart," Lisa shared with me.

"Oh that makes me so sad," I lamented, feeling sick that she had no one there to comfort her. "Why did she have all those boils? What do they do for them? Does she get any medical care?"

"Her orphanage is a state-run orphanage. It's not a nice place," Lisa said sorrowfully. "I just wanted to pick her up and take her with me. She is always so stoic."

"You know, I've had this feeling, since the first moment I saw her, that she wasn't in a good place. I've fervently prayed for protection over her," I revealed.

"Wow. Well, that was the Holy Spirit speaking to you because it is right on the money. I don't mean to upset you, but her orphanage is, and I have to be delicate here, it's a state-run orphanage, so the resources are slim, the workers are few, and the children are many. You need to keep praying those prayers."

"You better believe I will. I have been faithfully praying for her every single day since June 16, 2011, and I will continue to pray for her. I pray for her health, our relationship, I pray for her healing, I pray for her paperwork, I pray for the process, I pray for everything I can think of - all the people who come into contact with her paperwork and her case, everything. I need to know what the next steps are. I'm determined to get her home in record time," I declared.

"That's amazing! Well, I'd say your prayers are working because we've never seen a case move through Hyderabad the way Munni's case is moving. We are still shocked at how quickly you got NOC. We've never seen NOC issued in 24 hours of Article 5. I think God is answering your prayers. The next step to pray about is your court affidavit. We need this to file your case in court. Did Heather explain to you that Hyderabad requires two trips? You will have to attend court."

"She did. And you will never believe this. I just found out that I received the full grant for the combined June/July grant selection from Gift of Adoption - they awarded me $7500.00!"

"Oh my goodness, that is amazing," Lisa agreed.

"God continues to blow me away. I know He has incredible plans for sweet Munni," I mused.

"Well, I'm not going to argue that at all. And whatever prayers you are praying, keep praying them, because God is definitely using them to move mountains. It's incredible. I've worked in India for twenty years, and Hyderabad specifically is maddening to work with because it's extremely difficult. Munni's progress is truly miraculous."

"Hearing this only motivates me more, Lisa. I'm going to have bloody knees praying for this court affidavit, and it will be a joy!"

"I don't doubt you for one second," Lisa affirmed, "and I'll join you in those prayers. Hopefully, we'll have that court affidavit in your hands very soon."

"I agree!"

We talked for a little while longer about the rest of the process. After we hung up, I thanked God for Lisa and her heart for Munni. I sat there, stunned that Lisa had met Munni several times over the course of several years. She has seen her change from a three-year-old to a six-year-old. The last several months, it began to sink in that I lost so much time with Munni, time I would never get back. It weighed heavy on my heart. As I reflected on my conversation with Lisa, once again, the shock of how God orchestrated the pieces of this adoption overwhelmed me. He led me, using a stranger online, to the agency whose caseworker was also adopting a little girl from Munni's exact orphanage, and whose referral picture accidentally included Munni. Then, that agency's India program director just happened to have multiple interactions with Munni every year since Munni entered the orphanage. She has videos and pictures of Munni from several of those interactions. She advocated for Munni for years, praying that a family would come forward for this precious child. Tears streamed down my face as I humbly thanked God for choosing me to be Munni's mom, that I was the one who got to see this incredible, miraculous story unfold before my very eyes. My whole body tingled. Excitement filled my entire being as I thought about the months to come. I knew I was on the verge of watching God perform the greatest miracle yet in this adoption journey.

* * * * *

Another school year had started. This was the fourth September since I began my adoption journey. I thought back to 2009 when I sat on my front porch and heard God whisper, ever so sweetly, that living with me would be a thousand times better than living in an orphanage. It was hard to believe that I almost allowed my singleness to rob me of this pilgrimage. I was not the same fearful girl who waited with wringing hands and wore a scarlet letter of single shame.

No, God used this sojourn to completely transform me. He stripped away the fear that once paralyzed me, and He replaced it with a faith that continued to prevail through the storms, floods, and fire. He proved to me, time and time again, I can have hope in Him, and He will sustain me. He gave me a touchstone when He quietly spoke the Genesis verse to me - is anything too hard for the Lord?[8] My faith had grown with each answered prayer and every step forward, my faith doubled and tripled in size, moving like a giant avalanche. My metamorphosis showed a girl with thin faith and timid prayers revolutionize into a mom boldly fighting for my daughter like a wild, rabid dog proclaiming God's promises every step of the way. I was not stopping until she was home.

I relentlessly prayed for the court affidavit to be issued in record time. Lisa joined me in praying for a miracle, but warned me that many times, the affidavits are rift with typos and the corrections set back the process weeks, even months. I determined I would pray against human inefficiency and pray for God's protection over her affidavit.

The last week of September, Lisa emailed me with the news I had been waiting for - the affidavit arrived at the agency. And lo and behold, there was only one typo. It was a minor one that had absolutely no bearing on my information so there was no need for revision. Glory Hallelujah! I was ecstatic. She was assembling other documents and a list of instructions. She told me that she would send me another email when she sent it to the courier. I was on cloud nine. The thought that Munni could be home by Christmas was starting to look like a reality. I was becoming cautiously optimistic.

Saturday morning at 10 a.m., my doorbell rang. My dogs barked wildly as I ran to the front door. I barely caught a glimpse of the FedEx guy as he jumped into his truck and sped off to his next destination. I looked down at my welcome mat to see another glorious envelope just waiting for me to scoop it into my arms. I bent down, picked it up, and held it to my chest. I closed my eyes and thanked God for answering all of my prayers that I had prayed over these documents. I thought about all of the hands that had touched these papers: from the person who typed it up to the person who stuffed it into an envelope in India, to the courier services and sorting facilities in India, to the airlines, to all of the sorting that happened once the plane landed in the United States, to the mail sorting facility at the courier stateside. I thought of all the process again to get it to my agency and then back across the country to my front doorstep. What a miracle.

I carefully opened the envelope and pulled out the unique mint green paper on which my court affidavit was typed. I looked over the instructions Lisa included and glanced at my watch. I calculated that I could accomplish everything and get this package back to FedEx by noon. That would guarantee its arrival back to Lisa by Monday. I got ready, grabbed everything I needed for my errands, and headed out the door. I was a woman on a mission.

At 12:10 p.m., I emailed Lisa that she should receive the affidavit and other required items by early Monday afternoon. Nothing on my end would be responsible for any delay. I prayed for protection over the package, and for a swift process.

CHAPTER 20
DECEMBER 2012

More than two months had passed since my court affidavit was returned to India. It was the first week of December. Every day that I didn't receive a phone call or email about my court date only exacerbated the situation. My patience grew paper thin and my frustration was like an active volcano, ready to blow at any moment. I was on edge. I hated being so close to the end and still feeling completely out of control and not knowing anything.

On my way home from school Tuesday, December 4, my cell phone rang. I quickly glanced at the caller ID. It was my agency. I quickly answered.

"Hello, Kristen." I heard Lisa's friendly voice. "I think this is the call you've been waiting for!"

"No!" I shrieked. "Do I have a court date?"

"Well, kind of," Lisa laughed. "We are waiting to confirm it tomorrow morning, so I don't want you to buy your tickets just yet. But, could you leave Friday morning? Your attorney thinks your court date will be December 12."

My heart stopped. "What?"

"She thinks your court date will be December 12," Lisa repeated.

I started laughing through the tears, "LISA! I can't believe this."

"I know. It's like you wait and wait, and then, all of the sudden, BAM! You are moving." she replied.

"No! I mean, you are not going to believe this. Way back when I started my adoption journey, when I sent in my application to the Nepal program, I prayed for a due date. He whispered December 12."

"Oh my goodness," Lisa gasped.

"When Nepal closed, and December 2010 came around, I was so depressed and bitter and twisted. I thought maybe I heard Him wrong or it was a figment of my imagination. That date has haunted me ever since. It took root in my heart, and I've always wondered about it. When you just told me that, I can't describe the emotions that swept through me. I'm in shock." I wept into my phone.

"That's amazing, Kristen!"

"Wait, and you said that I should be prepared to leave on Thursday? That is crazy. Oh my goodness. I have so much to do!" I started to freak out, thinking of all that needed to happen before I could leave the country. I had lesson plans to make, care plans for my dogs, packing. Full panic mode set in.

"We would like for you to leave on Thursday so that you have a few days with Munni before court. Once court happens, you will have to take her back to the orphanage. I know it's cutting it close time wise, but I really want you to have that bonding time with her. You've waited so long."

My throat tightened thinking about spending three glorious days with Munni. "I will do whatever it takes to get those days with her," I managed. "I can't even imagine being in the same room with her, touching her, hugging her!"

"I'm thrilled for both of you, Kristen! I'm praying so much. Start calling about flights. See if you can put some on hold. I will call you tomorrow as soon as I hear from the attorney," Lisa assured me.

"Okay, I will. I'm going to have a busy night," I laughed.

"Indeed you are," she agreed.

I hung up the phone and screamed. WOW! God continued to do wondrous and miraculous feats every step of this journey. Still stunned, I drove the rest of the way home wondering how in the world I could pull everything off in the next forty-eight hours. As soon as I walked into my house, I sat down and wrote out a few lists. I made three categories: school, packing, home. Then, I texted my friends for help. I knew there was no way I could do this on my own. I called my mom.

"Hi, Sweetie," she answered.

"Mom," I stared crying.

"What's wrong?" she asked worried.

"I'm going to India. Thursday," I replied through my tears.

"THURSDAY! Kristen! This is wonderful. Oh my goodness. Talk about short notice. When did you find out?" she asked.

"Just a few minutes ago. Can you please come over and help me? I'm so overwhelmed."

"Of course. I'm on my way!" she hung up the phone before I could even say goodbye.

Twenty minutes later, my mom opened my front door. "You're on your way to India!" she exclaimed.

"Hi Mom!"

"Well, operation get your bags packed is underway it looks like," my mom observed as she glanced around at the luggage I had brought up from the basement.

"I'm so overwhelmed. I don't even know where to start. I have so much to do. Will you go to Target with me? I don't even have everything I need for her!" my heart rate accelerated at the thought of seeing her in just a few short days. But then panic set in when the mile long lists of tasks awaited my attention before I could step foot on the plane. There didn't seem to be enough time to accomplish all that needed to be done. I prayed for supernatural strength and laser sharp focus.

My mom and I each grabbed a cart and headed toward the little girls' section. Up to this point, by miraculous self-control, I had only allowed myself to buy Munni two dresses I found on sale when I got NOC. Besides those dresses, I had nothing for her. No clothes, no pajamas, no shoes, no underwear, no toys, no socks, nothing. Based on what Lisa had told me about the orphanage, I knew they shared clothing. She had nothing of her own. Maybe it was right, maybe it was wrong, but I wanted to spoil her and bring her beautiful, new clothes she could call her own. Clothes that would be worn for the first time by her. I couldn't wait to see her face as she looked at her pretty new dresses, her shoes, her hair accessories. I envisioned painting her fingernails and little toes. I pictured rubbing scented lotion on her beautiful, scarred arms and legs. I saw myself putting giant, obnoxious, pink bows in her short hair. I imagined all of this as I looked as the sweetest little dress hanging on a hanger, and I could feel my emotions rising to the surface. All of the years of longing for my daughter, the sorrow I almost drown in when Nepal closed, the electric current that shot through my body when

I saw Munni's precious face for the very first time, the panic and fear I felt when India suspended adoptions, the despair and sorrow that returned when I didn't have the money to start her adoption and my dad refused to help me, the joy and elation I felt when Help Us Adopt granted me the money and got the ball rolling, the healing and restoration that happened in my relationship with my dad, the unprecedented movement of her case in that particular area of India, the unremarkable full grant from Gift of Adoption that would cover the two trips I had to make to Hyderabad, all of the prayers, the tears, the words of encouragement from others, the longing, the hoping - all of it - erupted in uncontrollable, heaving sobs in the middle of Target. I could not stop. I fell into my mom's embrace and wailed. Concerned shoppers asked my mom if they needed to call for help. She politely told them they were witnessing tears of relief and joy; I was about to meet my daughter after years of waiting.

A few hours later, we arrived back at my house. A massive migraine loomed at the base of my neck, anxiety and fear took over as I did not have time for a migraine attack. I had too much to do. My mom encouraged me to take my medicine and go to bed. She reasoned if I got a good night's rest with my prescription medication, I could face tomorrow with renewed energy. She said a prayer for me and left. Even though my mind raced with all that still needed to be accomplished, I took her advice, swallowed my pill, and headed to bed.

The next day, Lisa did not call. Instead of going to work, I writhed in pain in my bed. Simon laid next to me, offering comfort the only way he knew how. My efforts to avoid a colossal attack proved useless; this migraine was a ten on the Richter scale. I was supposed to leave for India the next day, but it would be impossible. In addition, I had yet to hear from Lisa. I hadn't purchased plane tickets. I hadn't packed. I hadn't completed lesson plans. The migraine annihilated me for two solid days.

Late Thursday afternoon, my phone rang. It was Lisa. My head pounding, and what felt like an ice pick penetrating my brain through my eyeball, I gingerly picked up my phone and answered, "Hello?"

"Hey there, are you okay? You sound sick," she asked worried.

"I have the worst migraine. It started a few hours after we talked on Tuesday," I answered.

"Oh no! That's awful," Lisa lamented, "well, I'm sorry I didn't call you yesterday. The attorney didn't confirm your court date until today. I'm sorry, Kristen, but it's not going to be December 12."

"You know what? I couldn't make that if I tried. This migraine completely wiped me out. I haven't been able to do anything. Even though I wanted that date more than anything, obviously, it's not going to happen," I accepted.

"I'm sorry you've been so sick. Migraines are horrible, completely debilitating."

"Thank you. Does the attorney have a date?" I asked.

"She does! Your court date is December 19. Do you think you could get there by next Saturday?" Lisa wondered.

"Oh my goodness!" a renewed excitement filled my mind, "I can definitely get there by then! I feel such relief knowing I have a week or so to prepare. This changes my whole frame of mind. I feel like I can breathe," I responded as I felt my shoulders relax.

"Okay, great. Why don't you start looking at flights. Once you get your flights booked, send me the information. Minal will book your room at the hotel. It's close to the orphanage and very comfortable. I'm going to send you an email with travel information, details about the court process, and other general information about the trip. Read it over and let me know if you have any questions. Don't forget, send me your flight info as soon as you have it booked. I'm thrilled for you, Kristen!" Lisa exclaimed.

Excitement bubbled in my heart, "I can't believe I'm finally going to meet her!"

"You've waited long enough. And so has Munni," Lisa declared.

My dad pulled up to the curb in the dark of the early morning. It was 3:30 am and the airport was near desolate. My first flight to Chicago wasn't until 5:30 am, but since it was an international flight, my dad insisted we arrive the full two hours prior to departure. He didn't want me to miss my flight. My parents helped me unload my luggage from the car. My dad called the porter over and tipped him to take care of my bags. Then, he asked him to take a photo of us. We talked about my flight details for the umpteenth time, and I hugged my parents and thanked them.

"Now, you're going to Skype us once you get to the hotel, right?" my dad asked.

"Yep. I will arrive Saturday night, but that's going to be Saturday morning your time. I'll be 10 and a half hours ahead of you," I assured him.

"Okay. And when do you meet Munni?" he asked me again.

"I meet her on Monday!" I couldn't contain the excitement in my voice.

"Oh, Kristen!" my mom said, "I can't wait to see her!"

"So, you're going to Skype us once you get her back to the hotel room with you, right?" my dad questioned me again.

"I promise that you will be the first people I Skype once I have her back at the hotel," I smiled as I thought about how much my dad's heart had changed.

"Okay. Be careful. We love you," he said as he gave me a final hug.

"Love you, Sweetie. We are praying for you and for sweet Munni," my mom told me as she hugged me goodbye.

"I love you," I told my parents as I waved goodbye and walked into the airport. This day was finally here. I was about to board a plane to meet my precious daughter. It felt surreal.

I walked up to the ticket counter and handed my passport to the ticketing agent.

"Good morning. Where we headed today?" he casually asked.

A smile spread across my face, "India!"

CHAPTER 21
MEETING MUNNI

I woke before the alarm sounded. Excitement made sleep nearly impossible. I opened my eyes and joy immediately flooded my heart. Today was the day I would finally meet Munni! Minal had left a message at the front desk informing me that we would depart for the orphanage at 10 am. Giddy with anticipation, I could barely keep myself together as I ate my breakfast and got ready. Right before I headed down to the lobby to meet Minal, I recorded a quick video message to Munni. In it, I professed my deep love and longing for her and shared how many, many people were praying for us. I grabbed my bag, the iPad, my camera, and headed out the door. As soon as I saw Minal in the lobby, I started to cry. At long last, this day had arrived. I couldn't contain the tears of joy and relief any longer. Minal comforted me and told me to sit down while she went in search of a box of tissues. Meanwhile, the hotel manager came over to see if everything was okay. I quickly explained that I was adopting my daughter and that my tears were tears of joy because today was the day I finally got to meet her. She looked at the necklace I wore around my neck and asked me, "Is Munni her name?"

"It is! It's the most beautiful name!" I gushed.

"It's very clear how much you love your daughter," she responded, "it's a beautiful thing what you are doing."

"Thank you," I cried, "I have waited a very long time for this moment, and I'm completely overwhelmed with emotion."

"We are very happy for you and Munni. Will she be coming back to the hotel with you?" she questioned.

"Yes! She will be with me for three days until the court hearing," I answered.

By this time, Minal came back with a box of tissues and a declaration that sent my heart racing. "Kristen, the car is out front waiting for us."

I gathered my things and walked out of the lobby with Minal. We looked at each other and she smiled at me as we got in the car.

"The day is finally here!" Minal declared.

"I can't believe it! It feels like a dream. Is the orphanage far from here?" I asked.

"No, only about 15 minutes with traffic," she responded.

I sat back and looked out the window at the world around me. I watched the people going about their day, thinking how odd life is: It kept humming along while my whole world was about to change in the best way possible. I wondered if Munni knew I was coming for her today? Did they tell her anything at all? I had sent a photo book with Heather when she went for her court process for her daughter. Although I knew it had been delivered to the caretakers at the orphanage, I couldn't help but wonder if anyone read it to her or even let her look at it.

What seemed like only a few moments later, the car pulled up to a massive iron gate. Minal spoke in Hindi to the guard and he pushed a button. The black and gold ornate gates slowly opened. The car pulled in and started its way down a long, dusty, bumpy dirt road. To the left, were pinkish buildings. Minal informed me that was where the administrative offices were housed. The car continued its course down the road. I noticed rubbish everywhere, old newspapers flying in the wind. Yellow street dogs laid sunning themselves amongst the rubble. A woman wearing a bright pink sari walked in the cloud of dust; she appeared immune to the scene around her. The car followed the bend in the road, pulled over to the shade of a tree, and parked. I looked out the other side and saw old, rusted playground equipment. The tattered swing set seemed lonely with two chains that hung from the metal cross pole but ended in emptiness instead of a seat. Where there should have been three swings, only one remained. Did Munni ever swing there? It was depressing to look at the pretense of what was supposed to bring joy to children. Gazing at the surroundings, I felt incredibly sad. This is what Munni saw every single day. This was her world.

We got out of the car and walked up to the entrance of the orphanage. We took off our sandals and walked inside. I held my breath. This was were

Munni lived, where she slept, played, ate, bathed, made friends, passed all of her days. We walked into what appeared to be a lobby area. The black floor tile seemed inappropriate and ominous for an orphanage. There were several chairs, a bench, and a sofa. A huge, rectangular fish tank displayed murky water with goldfish slowly swimming in their contained environment. A large, golden bust of some important dignitary sat perched on a pedestal. It was positioned to be in the direct line of vision as soon as one stepped inside the orphanage. I wondered who it was and why he was so important. Next to the sofa was a smaller, wooden desk. A plump, friendly-faced, woman dressed in a brilliantly-colored sari sat behind it, obviously conducting important business. The phone rang and she answered speaking quickly in her native language. From the outside, it seemed a spirited conversation. Other women stood around waiting, while a few more attended to cleaning tasks. An old, wrinkled woman bent down and swept the floor with what looked like a homemade broom. Her job seemed endless as new dust managed to instantly appear on the black tile.

Minal walked up to the woman holding court at the wooden desk. They chattered and laughed casually. I heard Munni's name several times. Minal walked back to me and told me the woman with whom she spoke was the second in charge of the orphanage. The night before, Minal had told me to make a list of questions that I wanted to ask the orphanage. She said it would be my only chance to possibly find out any information, but warned me that many times, the orphanages don't reveal any extra details that weren't already included in the child's medical and social report. For Munni, both of her reports were thin and missing tons of information. Multiple questions in a row on each file were left blank, as if the person filling it out couldn't be bothered to take the time to complete it. Minal told me to take out my list and walk to the desk with her.

"Sanjeeta, this is Kristen Williams. She is adopting Munni," Minal introduced me.

"Namaste, Kristen," she replied.

"Namaste," I responded with my hands, palms together, in front of me.

"Munni had an exam today, so she is at school. I sent an ayah to bring her back here," Sanjeeta informed me.

An exam? For a 6-year-old? I found it strange, didn't they realize I would be here today? They really take education seriously, I thought to myself.

"Kristen has some questions about Munni if you have time to answer them?" Minal asked Sanjeeta.

"Of course, I will try to help you the best I can," she responded.

I unfolded the paper and handed it to Sanjeeta. I felt a good vibe from her; I could tell she was a warm person. "I wrote these down. I don't know if you have all of the information, but anything you do know would be greatly appreciated," I pleaded with her.

Sanjeeta looked at my questions and let out a sigh. Then, she proceeded to answer each question I had written down, filling in the gaps of the unknown. With each successive question she answered that revealed more information about Munni's history, I had to fight back tears. My heart shattered thinking about all that my precious daughter had experienced in her short life.

After she answered the last question, Sanjeeta folded up my paper, took a moment of silence, and then looked directly at me. "Munni was horribly tortured before she came to us," she said with tears in her eyes, "and shortly after her arrival here, she stopped talking. She didn't speak for an entire year. What she endured - well, there are no words," she lamented.

Suddenly, the air felt thick and I found it harder to breathe. I couldn't hold the tears any longer. I let them fall.

"We are very happy that you are adopting her. It is clear the love you have for her," Sanjeeta admitted.

I nodded my head because my throat was too tight to form any coherent words. All I wanted to do was to pull Munni into my arms and hug her for eternity.

"Kristen," Minal interrupted my grieving, "I am going to step outside to make phone calls about some other cases. Are you okay to wait here?"

"It's not a problem," I replied, soaking in every single detail of this place Munni had called home for the last three and a half years.

As Minal walked out the door, an Indian couple walked in. Huge smiles spread across their faces as they walked to the desk where Sanjeeta sat. They conversed in a jovial manner, everyone laughing. After a few moments, the couple sat down on the sofa next to the chair where I was seated. In broken English, the woman timidly asked me, "You adopt child?"

"Yes!" I replied, trying to focus on the joy that awaited me when Munni came back from school.

"We adopt!" she told me excitedly.

"That's fantastic!" My face lit up with happiness for this couple. I was somewhat stunned because I knew that adoption was still very much taboo in the Indian culture, but this couple was obviously very excited about their new child.

An ayah approached us from the long hallway, a gorgeous baby girl in her arms. She walked over to the couple. They both jumped up and smiled at each other. The woman took the baby into her arms and immediately cradled her. An aura of joy surrounded these new parents, and I felt myself getting choked up with emotion once again. Another family formed by adoption, it was marvelous. They all talked excitedly and surrounded the beautiful, baby girl. I felt privileged that I witnessed such an extraordinary event.

About an hour later, Minal came back inside. She informed me that Munni would be arriving shortly. My heart raced with excitement. I wanted Minal to film this once in a lifetime moment, so I went over how to video on the iPad once again. I wanted to ensure that this moment would be captured forever. After my technology lesson, she asked me for the bag of saris I had purchased for the caregivers. She pulled out the fabric to show Sanjeeta. I held my iPad in my hand and listened to the bustling conversation in a tongue I didn't understand. All of the sudden, I heard Munni's name being said in surprised, happy tones. I turned around to see her standing next to an ayah. They slipped through the back instead of coming in the front door.

"Oh my goodness!" I squealed as I quickly handed my iPad to Minal and ran around the chair to get to where they were standing. I fell to my knees in front of her. Time seemed to stand still; I thought my heart was going to explode out of my chest! She was gorgeous! She stood in her green, plaid school uniform and smiled down at me. "Hi, Munni!" I greeted her with unbridled enthusiasm. She smiled back. Everything about her was perfect. The sweet dimple on her right cheek, those deep, penetrating black eyes, and her crooked little smile. I breathed it all in as I took her hands into mine and kissed them. She giggled in reply. I didn't want to freak her out, but all I wanted to do was hold her. I opened my arms in the gesture of a hug and asked her if I could hug her. Even though she didn't understand what I was saying, she understood my non-verbal communication and nodded her head as she gingerly leaned towards me. I wrapped my arms around her thin body and squeezed her with all the love I had. In that moment, I was transported to a place of pure ecstasy and perfection. Nothing would have made that moment any more perfect. My daughter was in my arms. My daughter. I held her close to me and whispered in her ear, "I love you, Munni." After the initial shock of finally seeing her in real life wore off, I stood up and asked if she wanted to sit on my lap as I gestured towards the chair. I took her green backpack off of her back, stunned at how heavy it was. It had to weigh more than her! We walked to the chair and I sat down and pulled her onto my lap. I could not stop smiling if my life depended on it - here I was with my daughter, sitting on my lap. I was in heaven. I opened a bag of gummy bears and offered her some. She excitedly took an orange one and smiled as she popped it into her mouth. I reveled in this moment.

The woman who came back with them from the school walked over to us and said something to Munni in a forceful tone. I didn't understand but Munni bobbed her head back and forth in typical South Indian fashion. The woman spoke again. Then, in an instant that happened too quickly to understand, the woman slapped Munni across the face. Horrified at what had just occurred, I pulled Munni closer to me. It was an extremely tricky situation. I didn't know who this woman was but I knew that I had to leave Munni here after court. I didn't want my reaction to have a negative impact on her for the rest of the time she would be in this place, without my supervision and protection. Every ounce of my body raged against the woman for slapping my daughter while she sat on my lap. Had this occurred in the United States, it would not have been a pleasant outcome for this woman. Fire shot out of my eyes as I declared, "She's fine sitting here with me."

Minal didn't see what happened but heard my terse reply and hurried over to find out what happened. She informed me that the abusive woman was Munni's school teacher. More anger pulsed through my body as I thought of the injustice of this. If she felt so free to slap Munni across the face while sitting on my lap, who knows what she does to the children in the classroom? Recovered from the sting of the slap, Munni started counting in English. The woman approached us again, this time I pulled Munni close in a protective manner. The teacher pushed Munni's arm as if to tell her to continue counting. I assume she wanted to show me that Munni knew her numbers in English, but I was completely appalled at her violent tendencies. I congratulated Munni on her English and gave her more gummy bears. Minal ran interference and distracted the teacher with conversation and led her away from us. I reached into my bag and pulled out a pair of hot pink sunglasses that I bought for her. As I handed them to Munni, her whole face lit up in excitement. She put them on immediately. I laughed at how beautiful and perfect she was. Minal came back, took a few pictures of us together, and handed me my iPad.

The mean woman beckoned Munni once again. I looked at Minal with pleading eyes; I didn't want this lady anywhere near Munni. Minal informed me that the person in charge of signing off on the custody papers for me to take Munni was not on the campus. We would have to come back. The teacher, who apparently also worked at the orphanage, summoned Munni back to the room to change out of her school clothes and eat lunch. My heart sank. I did not want to walk out of that orphanage without Munni. Begrudgingly, I motioned for Munni to hop off of my lap. I hugged her again and kissed her on the cheek. I asked Minal to relay to Munni that I would be back for her shortly. Minal spoke to Munni and she bobbled her head in response. Then, she turned, took the teacher's hand, and walked down the long hallway. I watched with a deep yearning: All I wanted to do was run down that hallway, grab Munni, and bring her with me. Instead, I gathered up my things and walked out the door with Minal.

As we drove back down the long, bumpy driveway, Minal told me we would grab lunch to help pass the time. She thought by time we finished eating, the woman who needed to sign the custody papers would be back. Feeling deflated, I tried to feign excitement about lunch. The car approached the massive iron gates once again. From this perspective, I felt like we were being released from prison. Right as the guard went into the guardhouse to open the gate, a woman in a tangerine-colored sari came running out from the administrative complex, waiving a paper in her hand. Minal opened her window and conversed with the woman. Turning to me with a smile on her face, she told me, "Today is your lucky day, Kristen. Parvati is back in the building and ready to sign the custody papers."

"No way!" I screamed in excitement. What a miracle. The driver pulled the car over to the side and we quickly got out. We followed the lady who flagged us down back through a maze of buildings and into a room at the end of an open air corridor. We walked in and were greeted by several woman. I looked around at the office space. The women were typing on typewriters. It was as if I had been transported back in time. The walls were decorated by giant floor to ceiling columns of green legal folders, none of them marked. A fan slowly turned as if it had surrendered to the heat, knowing its rotations wouldn't bring any relief.

Minal introduced me to Parvati. Strikingly beautiful and tall, she greeted me with an affectionate smile. She walked over to one of the columns and pulled out a green, unmarked folder. She laid it on the table and opened it. I realized it was Munni's folder. She took out a piece of paper and handed it to me. Minal instructed me to sign and date it and then I handed it back to her. Parvati signed the document and put it back into Munni's folder, then tossed the folder onto a nearby desk. I looked back at the columns and my mouth dropped open. All of those files were the children at the orphanage. I knew her orphanage was one of the largest, since it was state-run, but I couldn't mask my shock at the number of files or the haphazard filing system. I silently thanked God for bringing me to this point in the process. No wonder Hyderabad was an extremely difficult region with which to work. How in the world did they ever find a child's file with the way this office was set up? I realized in that moment that getting Munni home was truly a miracle. Minal and Parvati chatted a few moments more. Then, she called down to the orphanage and relayed the message that we were coming back to take Munni with us. I tried to remain patient while they finished their friendly conversation. At last, Minal turned to me and asked, "Are you ready to get your daughter?"

The car couldn't drive fast enough; I was quite certain that I could have beat it had I walked back down to the orphanage. Finally, the driver pulled over to shade spot and parked. I exercised serious self-control and didn't bolt out of the door as soon as it stopped, even though every part of me wanted to run in there as quickly as I could. We walked in and greeted Sanjeeta. She called for an ayah to bring Munni up to the lobby. My heart pounded in my chest so loud I could hear it. It seemed like forever, but a few minutes later, Munni came walking down the hallway, holding the hand of an ayah. Dressed in a beautiful, beaded dress, she smiled when she saw me. My heart melted into a puddle. I walked quickly towards her and took her hand in mine. Nothing felt more perfect in that moment! We headed out the door and climbed into the car. I motioned for Munni to sit on my lap. She looked hesitant, then acquiesced and scooted over to my side and sat on my lap. I folded my arms around her and smelled her hair. I was in heaven. The driver pulled away and headed back towards the massive iron gates. After we turned the bend in the road, I saw the couple who were adopting the beautiful baby walking along the dirt driveway. Neither one of them held a baby; instead, they trudged along with empty arms. The woman wept as she walked with her husband, who stared blankly into the road, clearly distressed. I didn't understand. I pointed to them and told Minal about my interaction with them at the orphanage. Minal's face grew somber and she proceeded to tell me, "It's a very unfortunate situation, Kristen."

"What do you mean? They were thrilled when the baby was placed in their arms," I told her.

"As you know, adoption isn't fully embraced in India the way it is in the United States," Minal reminded me, "and in this case, the mother-in-law came and she didn't approve of the adoption."

"Who cares? Didn't they want the baby?" my naivety exposed.

"If the mother-in-law doesn't approve of the adoption, they can't move forward. That is part of the culture," Minal educated me.

I sat in shock. Heartbroken for the couple, I couldn't imagine the pain they felt. I thought back to the resistance I once received from my dad. I never let that stop me. I wondered how different my outcome would have been had I not lived in the United States. I felt sick to my stomach for them. Once again, I thanked God for walls He tore down and the transformation that occurred in my dad's heart. I hugged Munni tighter, realizing that a miracle sat on my lap.

CHAPTER 22
GETTING TO KNOW HER

We arrived back at the hotel and pulled up to the elegant entrance. I watched Munni's face as she took it all in; her eyes filled with fascination and wonder, I couldn't believe that I was the one who got to witness these firsts with her! I held her hand as we walked through the lobby. The hotel manager quickly ran up to us and excitedly welcomed us back to the hotel. All I wanted to do was get to our room so we could finally be alone and get to know one another. The manager kept begging me to take Munni to the pool, show her around the grounds, and get her something to eat. Annoyed, I told her that I just got Munni and we were exhausted and wanted to head back to the room to relax. Finally, the manager relented and let us go on our way. Minal agreed with me that the manager needed some lessons in hospitality with regard to not being so pushy.

We got off the elevator, and Minal retired to her room. She told me to call if I needed anything; but mostly, she wanted us to enjoy our time together. Munni and I walked towards my room and I got out the keycard to open the door. I handed it to her. She looked up at me with questioning eyes. I pointed to the slot in the door and motioned for her to put the card in the slot. Munni slid the card into the slot and the door blinked green and we heard the unlocking of the door. Munni squealed and clapped her hands. I opened the door. She walked in and looked around at the king-sized bed and the giant window that looked out onto the green lawn below. Pure wonder filled her eyes as she meticulously cased the room for every new detail. It took maybe five minutes before she located the remote and accidentally pushed buttons that led to turning on the T.V. She gasped when the picture came on the screen. She was in awe. She explored the room and bathroom. Things seemed to be going well, so I decided I would apply the lice treatment. Knowing that all of the children in the orphanage had lice, I did not want to get it. Heather shared how when she brought her daughter back to the hotel, the next morning the pillow was covered in black specks from lice. That was enough for me to institute the lice treatment as quickly as possible.

I opened the kit and put on the plastic gloves. I called Munni over and motioned for her to sit on the bed. I carefully began to apply the shampoo. My stomach dropped as I saw all of the scars on her scalp. Every picture I had of her was taken from the front. I was not prepared to see what I saw. All over her head were what appeared to be burn scars. The largest one covered the crown of her head. It was the size of a baseball, lumpy, and bald. None of the scars grew any hair; it was clear these had been third degree burns that completely damaged not only the skin, but the hair follicles as well. Rage burned deep inside of me at the thought of the person who did these atrocious acts to my daughter. I fought back tears because I didn't want to upset Munni. Once all of her hair was drenched in the lice shampoo, I took off the gloves and set the timer on my phone. Munni sat on the edge of the bed with a sweet smile on her face. The amount of love I had for this child was immeasurable. I made an internal promise that I would never let anyone hurt her ever again. I stared at her, still in disbelief that we were finally together!

All of the sudden, the doorbell rang. I thought it was odd since Minal indicated we wouldn't see her until tomorrow. I walked to the door and opened it. The young hotel manager stood with a cart and two other hotel employees. On the cart, was a beautiful cake that read, "Welcome to the family, Munni!" I was stunned! In that moment, I realized that all of her prodding to take Munni around the hotel was an attempt to stall for time.

"Come in!" I exclaimed as I waved them into the room.

"We wanted to do something special for you and Munni on this momentous occasion!" the manager said cheerily.

"This is an incredible surprise!" I replied.

The other hotel worker wheeled the cart back to the table. They lit the candles while I picked up Munni to show her the cake. The manager handed Munni a knife to cut it and took several pictures of us. I was blown away by their thoughtfulness of such a kind gesture. They stood around while the manager asked me questions. The timer on my phone started dinging and saved me from a long conversation I didn't have the energy to have. I thanked them once again and ushered them out of the room. I didn't want to cause any more damage to her scalp, so I hurried to rinse it off of her. I helped her get undressed for the shower. As I took her clothes off, her tiny body revealed permanent marks of the horrible abuse Sanjeeta told me she had suffered. I almost vomited. Acutely aware that Munni was watching me, I prayed for strength to hold myself together as I viewed the landmine of purposeful scars that riddled her thin body. I forced a smile and led her to the bathroom. I turned on the water, took out the giant pink loofa, and poured the special scented body wash onto it. I motioned for Munni to stand under the water. She timidly walked into the shower and then burst out into laughter once the warm water rained down on her. I sudsed up the loofa and began washing her body. She giggled and squealed as she tried to jump in the puddle of water that formed on the shower floor. I stood up and rinsed all of the lice shampoo out of her hair. Watching her shriek with joy and dance in the shower made me laugh. She was having the time of her life, and I was thankful to witness another first.

After a while of playing in the shower, I turned off the water and grabbed the huge, fluffy towel. I wrapped her in it, picked her up, and carried her to the bed. Gently, I dried her off. I reached into my suitcase and pulled out a very special pair of pajamas. They were pink, white, and red with elephants dancing on the pants. The top had two elephants embroidered with their trunks entwined around each other. I hoped she would love them as much as I did. I turned around and showed them to her. She clapped her hands together and squealed. I took that as an affirmative. I grabbed the scented lotion and began to moisturize her precious body. As I rubbed the sweet smelling lotion into her beautiful, brown skin, I prayed for miraculous healing as I massaged each scar. But by the grace of God, I managed not to cry. I didn't want to ruin this moment for her. She was clearly happy and enjoying this night. I fought back the urge to puke as I worked the lotion into horrible scars on her hands and wrists. I couldn't even allow my mind to wander for a second imagining the horrors she suffered. Seeing her scars evoked emotions in me I didn't know I could possess.

I put her pajamas on her and gave her a hug. My heart was in a constant state of overflowing love. Next, I ordered room service, turned on the television, and got out my iPad. I wanted to look at the video of when we met. I opened up the pictures and quickly became heartbroken. Somehow in the rush of Munni sneaking in the back door of the orphanage and my handing over the iPad to Minal, the video command must have switched off. Instead of a beautiful video capturing the moment forever, there were only two photos. I tried not to get upset, but I was extremely discouraged. I had waited for that moment for years; all I had to show for it were two pictures. And to top it off, they were both blurry. I sighed. I knew everyone on social media were waiting for an update, so I posted the first picture of our meeting and made it Facebook official. Finally, the moment I met my daughter!

I looked at my watch and knew I could Skype my parents. I dialed their number. Munni sat next to me, snuggled in my arm. The screen went black and then my mom and dad appeared before our eyes. Munni giggled. My mom gasped when she saw us, put her hands to her mouth, and softly said, "Oh, Kristen! She's beautiful!" Overcome with emotion, both my mom and dad had tears in their eyes at the sight of Munni sitting next to me. What was once a huge prayer and a dream, was now a living, breathing, beautiful miracle perched right next to me on the bed. It was a spiritual moment.

We talked for a little bit, and I told them all about my flight, the orphanage, and the rest of the itinerary for the trip. Finally, we hung up so that I could make other calls. I Skyped my sister. She, too, cried at the sight of Munni with me. I divulged to her what I found when I undressed Munni. My sister immediately prayed for her, for healing and restoration, and that she would find wholeness in Christ. She prayed for me and for our relationship as mother and daughter. It was the encouragement I needed. I Skyped several more friends, each one bursting into tears once they saw Munni and me side by side.

After several hours of Skyping, I hung up exhausted. I changed into my pajamas and crawled into bed with Munni. What an incredible day it had been! I patted the sheet next me and she snuggled up under the blankets, nestled in the crook of my arm. It felt like heaven. I checked Facebook one last time before turning out the lights. I had a million notifications - everyone was ecstatic for our meeting! I scrolled through some of the comments people left on the photo of me on my knees in front of Munni. I stopped in my tracks when I saw Kristen Wiggins' comment. My skin tingled and I felt the Holy Spirit come over me. Tears of joy and thankfulness poured out and I couldn't stop. Munni looked at me concerned. I laughed and tried to explain to her. I kept repeating, "Happy tears! Happy tears!" as I pointed to my smile. What an incredible God He is! I was completely floored and I thought about the verse that His ways are not my ways[9]. His promises are true. Even when I couldn't see it, He knew. I looked at Kristen's comment once more and thanked God profusely:

Williams! The clock!!!!

I stared at the blurry picture. Even though it wasn't tack sharp, the emotion in the photograph was clearly evident. And in the background, at the top of the photo, just barely in the frame, hung the clock. The moment I first saw my daughter face to face, the clock struck twelve noon. December 12. God kept His promise. My due date came to fruition after all.

* * * * *

We woke up early Wednesday morning. Court day had finally arrived and I didn't want to miss an extra moment with Munni. On the long flight to India, I wondered what we would do together for three days. I wondered if we would get bored. What would we do? We didn't speak the same language so there was a part of me that was nervous about the time we would be spending together. Now that I had spent two full days with her, I couldn't imagine my life without her. It seemed like I only snapped my fingers and the days were gone. Why did the time pass by so quickly?

We spent the early morning hours snuggling and giggling with one another. I stared at her beautiful face, willing myself to memorize every single detail. We ate a great breakfast and then took a shower to get ready for our big day in court. Dressed in a sweet, pink Salmar Kameez I purchased in the mall the day before, Munni looked stunning. She wore the pink flip flops I brought, a pink flower in her hair, and finished her look with the bright pink sunglasses. I soon realized I had little fashionista for a daughter.

We met Minal in the lobby and then headed out to the car. It was a longer drive to the courthouse. On the way, Minal instructed me about what to do and say when I stood in front of the judge. She also warned me that we would be waiting for a long time. I brought snacks, a little notebook and pencil, and stickers for Munni. Minal advised me not to bring any electronics.

We arrived shortly before 10 am. Minal gave instructions to the driver and then she motioned us towards a giant tree in the center of the court complex. Motorcycles in rows ten deep blocked the entrance. We carefully weaved our way through the motorbike trap; I didn't want to start the domino effect by accidentally knocking over a bike. We reached the tree and sat down on the cement bench that encircled the massive tree trunk. The tree provided shade from the blistering sun. Minal told us we would wait under the tree until our case was assigned a court room.

Several long, hot hours passed before Minal finally reported back that we could move inside. We walked into the building and followed Minal down a long hallway. She instructed us to sit on the chairs that were placed outside of a room. We sat down and watched as a yellow dog ran through the hallway, casually looking for food scraps. I fanned myself to try and keep cool. The heat was intense. The waiting had been miserable, yet Munni did not complain or act out at all. I was shocked at her calm demeanor. Finally, after another hour or so, Minal beckoned us into the courtroom. She motioned for us to take seats in the back row. Munni and I made our way down the aisle and found two chairs. They were covered in thick plastic. I was thankful to be wearing a long skirt; I imagined how disgusting it would feel to sit on these chairs in shorts. I could almost hear my skin pull away from the hot plastic. I looked around the courtroom, in awe of the place that would legally declare Munni was my daughter.

A fan slowly turned. It made no difference in the suffocating heat that engulfed the room. White paint peeled from the wall. Outside, I heard the Islam call to prayer. I looked through the iron honeycomb window frames to see a black cat walking expertly along red, terra cotta roof tiles. It felt like a scene right out of an Indiana Jones movie. I watched as what I assumed was a court clerk bringing in armfuls of files. She heaved each stack onto the table set up in front of the judge's ornate bench. Another woman with a typewriter sat at the table, putting paper in the typewriter, with each new case that stepped before the judge. The court clerk took another huge stack of files and made her way out of the room. Astounded at the process, I wondered how my file never got lost. I watched this procession several times before Minal caught my attention and motioned us towards the door. We stood up and made our way to her. Standing in the hallway was Parvati, Minal, and another woman I did not know. Parvati greeted me warmly and then instructed me not to say anything to the judge.

A few moments later, Parvati scurried into the courtroom, signaling us to follow. She and the other woman from the hallway walked up to the desk with the typewriter. They stood facing the judge's bench. I picked up Munni and held her close to me. A large, stern woman wearing a black robe walked out of a door, up to the majestic, carved wooden chair, and sat down. Afraid to make full eye contact, I stole a glance out of the side of my eye. She looked exactly like Large Marge from the movie *Pee Wee's Big Adventure*. All of the sudden, I became nervous. Parvati addressed the judge in English; the judge replied in Telugu. Oh no, I thought. This is not a great beginning. I held Munni, closed my eyes, kissed her cheek, and prayed for favor. Parvati's English/Telugu conversation with the judge continued for about five minutes. I saw Parvati do the namaste greeting to the judge and deduced that our time in front of the judge was over. I quickly looked up at the judge. She locked eyes with mine and my heart stopped. Then, she smiled. I smiled back and kissed Munni on the cheek. My heart resumed its beating.

"Congratulations, Kristen. You have passed court!" Parvati declared.

A smile spread across my face and I could feel the tears coming. I couldn't believe it. Munni was legally my daughter! We quickly moved out of the courtroom and into the hallway. Minal hugged me and I thanked the women profusely. We waited thirty minutes longer for the bond to be filed and then we headed to the car. It felt like I was walking on air. As soon as we sat inside the car, my joy quickly vanished. Minal informed me that we would return to the hotel to freshen up and then I had to take Munni back to the orphanage per the custody agreement. Immediately, I felt as if I had been punched in the stomach. I held Munni on my lap and hugged her tight; I would have done anything to stop time.

CHAPTER 23
RETURN

We pulled through the massive iron gates and started down the long, bumpy dirt road. Off to the side, yellow dogs laid strewn about like discarded garbage. Dirty papers and piles of cement littered the landscape. Every so often, a green sprout emerged through the rubble. Even in the most unlikely of places, life could not be extinguished. My heart started racing, and I tried to take in deep breaths and slowly exhale. I resisted this moment with every fiber of my being as I hugged Munni tighter and used every ounce of resolve to restrain the sobs that I knew were ready to erupt. The car stopped in front of the entrance. I felt as if all of the air was sucked out of the car. I hugged Munni as tightly as I could. She woke up groggy, and she looked around. Immediately, her face changed at the recognition of the orphanage. She looked at me with questioning eyes, and my heart broke. We got out of the car, walked up to the porch, took off our shoes, and walked inside. I held her tiny hand in mine. I never wanted to let go. I begged Minal to ask someone to please explain to her that I would be coming back for her, that I was not leaving her, and that I had to wait on the court order to be released. Minal spoke Telugu to the director and asked her to relay the message to Munni. I didn't understand what the director said but I prayed that somehow, Munni's precious 6-year-old mind could comprehend what she was being told. Munni looked at the director as she spoke and bobbled her head in typical South Indian fashion. How could she possibly understand? This must all be so confusing to her. I desperately prayed that God would fill her heart with peace and understanding. The director called out, and an ayah came and took Munni back to her room while I filled out more paperwork. It was all a blur as the only thing I could think about was my daughter.

After what seemed like hours, I finished signing all of the papers, and it was time for us to leave. I told Minal I needed to see Munni one last time. We walked down the long hallway, past rooms of sweet, little, Indian faces staring back at us. I focused on the black cement floor as we continued towards her room. It smelled of antiseptic, and I could hardly breathe. Finally, we arrived at her door. I stepped inside to see all of the girls seated on a mat, lined up against the wall. A torn, lopsided curtain that dangled from a flimsy cafe rod, barely covered the bottom of the dirty window. Posters of fruits and vegetables acted as decor. The walls were painted white until about halfway down where they abruptly changed to muddy brown. The paint chipped in striations that almost resembled a pattern. In the corner, two cribs stood side by side with frayed blankets covering tiny, thin mattresses.

The children laughed as I entered the room, and the two ayahs conversed in Telugu. I scanned the faces until I saw her. There she was. Sitting against the wall wearing the white dress I bought her, the pink flower in her hair. Our eyes met and she smiled back at me. Stunning. I walked over and hugged her with all of my might. I heard giggles from the other little girls. I fought back the rage I felt for having to leave her here for two more months. My heart felt ripped torn but I forced myself not to cry because I didn't want to make it worse for her. I whispered in her ear, "I love you Munni. Mommy Munni forever!" I pulled back to look at her beautiful face and her smile grew wider. I melted as I held her face in my hands, and my heart broke when I kissed the scar on her forehead. I told her again how much I loved her. How was I ever going to walk away from her? How could I just leave her here? All I wanted to do was to take her hand in mine and run as fast as I could far, far away from this place.

Minal called to me and told me it was time to leave. I squeezed my eyes shut as I prayed for the strength to leave my daughter behind - an act no mother should ever have to do. I stood up and walked to the door. My heart raced as I turned around to take one last look at my sweet Munni sitting against the wall. The expression on her face will haunt me until the day I die. Confusion. Betrayal. Sadness. Anger. Her dark eyes pierced my heart.

Minal gently touched my shoulder and guided me out of the room. Tears streamed down my face as we walked down the long hallway and out of the orphanage. My ears ringing, my vision became myopic; the closer we got to the car, the harder it was for me to breathe. I opened the dusty, black door and sat down on the seat. I lost all control and collapsed into a pile of deep, heaving sobs; grief pouring out of me. Minal sat next to me and gently put her hand on my back. No words were spoken.

* * * * *

The driver pulled up to the entrance of the hotel. It took every ounce of energy to get out of the car; Munni's last look haunted me. All I wanted to do was get on a plane and go home because I didn't want to spend another moment in India without her. I trudged through the hotel lobby, bloodshot eyes from crying, and tear-stained cheeks. In the elevator, Minal broke the silence, "Kristen, why don't you relax for a little while and then let's meet in the bar to celebrate. What happened today is nothing short of a miracle - your entire process to adopt Munni has moved with speed that I've never seen in Hyderabad cases. It is only right to celebrate that you are officially mother and daughter."

"Okay," I answered reluctantly, "I know I should celebrate but I can't get the image out of my mind of the look Munni gave me before I left. I feel like I've betrayed her and I'm sure that's how she felt."

"I understand. But one day when she is older, you will explain this process to her and she will understand why you had to leave. I know that doesn't help your heart now, but take comfort that you are changing her life for the better. Let's meet downstairs in an hour. Does that give you enough time?" she offered.

"Yep. Besides, I don't want to sit in the hotel room with nothing to do. It only makes things worse. I'll see you in an hour," I replied as we got off the elevator and headed to our respective rooms. I opened the door and walked into emptiness, nothing about it felt right. I flopped on the bed and cried.

A little while later, I got up and washed my face. I sat down to check my email. As I scrolled the inbox, the subject and sender of one particular email stopped me cold. It was from Patty, the social worker from the original agency that listed Munni on their waiting list where I found her. The subject was simply titled, "Munni." I quickly opened the email:

Hi Kristen,

I spoke with you quite a while ago about a little girl in India named Munni. As you may already know, then the entire system in India changed and we were no longer able to place Munni. Just today, Munni showed up on our "shared" list of children that we are able to place. We have locked her referral just in case you are interested. Would you still be interested in learning more about Munni? Please give me a call when you have time.

Sincerely,

Patty

I couldn't believe my eyes! I knew Patty had a special affection for Munni and wanted her to find her forever family. I quickly replied, informing her that I was in India and we had just passed court - Munni was legally my daughter! But, fear rose in my heart wondering why Munni would still be listed on the website as available? I asked her if I should be concerned. She replied a few minutes later:

Kristen,

We are celebrating here in MN - with tears in our eyes! That Munni is with you is wonderful news and it means that this was all meant to be. We will take care of letting CARA know that they need to get YOUR GIRL off the shared list. I hope you enjoyed your time with her and you get your girl home as soon as possible. And I would love a photo.

Happy Holidays.

Patty

I sat in awe staring at my computer screen. I thought how my whole process with Munni was orchestrated by God, right down to this email. It had been over a year since I last communicated with Patty but God made sure she knew the end result - Munni found her forever family, and it was me! I looked down at my arm to the tattoo I had done to permanently remind me of God's faithfulness and power: Is anything too hard for the Lord?[10]

* * * * *

On our way to the airport, I looked out the dusty window at people living their lives; I forced myself to memorize the sights, sounds, and smells of India - my daughter's birth country. I had never seen a more colorful country and as depressing as some of the scenes were, life seemed to fight for triumph. I turned to Minal and asked, "Do you think the written court order will really take two months? Do you think it's at all possible that Munni will be my forever Valentine?"

"Oh, I don't know, Kristen," Minal responded, "but it is never wrong to have hope. And I will join you in that hope that Munni becomes your forever Valentine," she said with a smile.

I looked out the window and grinned. I already started counting down the days until I would have my daughter in my arms once again.

* * * * *

My body ached from sitting in the cramped airplane seat. The long flight home from India provided to be a torture chamber for my mind. I couldn't stop replaying the images of leaving Munni behind; it was the hardest thing I've ever had to do. My heart hurt with excruciating pain and I wondered how I would ever live through the next two months. The night before, my sister had texted and called me until I answered. Her friend who adopted siblings also had to leave her sons behind in Guatemala while the process finished. She called my sister and told her I would need all of the support I could get. She went through it with her husband; she couldn't imagine facing that pain by herself. My sister called and let me sob into the phone for two hours. It was the most unbearable pain I had ever felt. Everything about this part of the process made me sick. I wondered if it would have long-term effects on our relationship as mother and daughter? How could she not think I had abandoned her? Even if she slightly comprehended the process and what was happening, two months was a long time for a little girl to wait. I knew every day would be a battle against the torment of waiting for the written court order and her passport. After seeing the filing system at her orphanage and picturing the court clerk walking with pounds of files in her arms, I tried my hardest not to get discouraged. I needed a miracle. A miracle that her court file wouldn't get lost. A miracle that the people who are supposed to sign off on documents would do so in an expeditious manner. A miracle that her court order wouldn't be misplaced in transit to her orphanage or worse, get lost in the shuffle of all the unmarked files. A miracle that her passport would be issued in record time. I was more determined than ever to pray my way through this final phase of waiting and I believed with all of my heart that God would make a clear path for Munni to be my forever Valentine. It would take a miracle; but as I had been learning throughout my adoption journey, I was in the best place for Him to bring that miracle to fruition. I had no control over the situation and my dependence remained completely upon Him and His power.

The plane landed in its final destination. Even though I was home, a cloud hung over me. I knew a part of me was missing; I left my heart in that sterile, depressing room where Munni lived. There were still four days before Christmas, but I found I didn't have the same excitement that once surrounded the season. I wanted Munni with me. I didn't want her in that orphanage. I didn't want her in that school with the abusive teacher. I wanted her home, with me, where I could give her all of the love, safety, and tenderness she deserved.

I gathered my luggage and headed out the door in search of my parents who were supposed to be waiting for me. I took two steps before I heard my mom call my name. She and my dad stood next to my dad's car, parked with the hazards flashing. I quickly made my way to them and immediately broke down when my mom hugged me. My dad took my luggage and loaded it in the trunk. Then he turned to me, "I thought you would need a pick-me-up," as he pointed to the backseat of his car. I looked in the backseat window to find Simon, my Boxer, wagging his nub, staring intently at me.

"Oh Dad, you have no idea!" I responded as I walked to the car and opened the door to receive hundreds of licks from my beloved Boxer. "We'll get through this, won't we, buddy?" I said to Simon as I let him spoil me with his love.

CHAPTER 24
FOREVER VALENTINE

February 11 arrived, and still no sign of Munni's passport being issued. I received news that the court order finally reached her orphanage last week. I called Lisa every day, hopeful that one of the phone calls would end with the exciting news that her passport had been issued. Unfortunately, those events never transpired. The closer Valentine's Day came, the more panic filled my being as there continued to be no word about her passport.

I called Lisa again with the intention of pleading my case to travel despite the passport not being issued.

"Hello there," she answered on the second ring.

"Hey. It's me again," I joked, "Lisa, I know Munni is supposed to be my forever Valentine. Every time I pray about it, I am filled with overwhelming peace. I know her Family Day is supposed to be on the day that is notorious for celebrating love. I know this is God's final stamp of approval on her adoption. I just know it. I'm supposed to be there on Valentine's Day; I know deep within my being that's the day I'm supposed to take her out of that horrendous place forever," I declared over the phone.

"Well, I'm not one to argue against God. If you really feel that's what the Holy Spirit is telling you, I can't stop you. But, you have to be prepared for the unknown circumstances. It's quite possible that her passport still won't be issued before you arrive. The last I checked this morning, it hadn't been released," Lisa informed me.

"I'm willing to take that risk. I know I'm supposed to get her on Valentine's Day," I emphasized again.

"Have you looked at flights at all?" she asked.

"I have some on hold. You give me the okay, and I'm hanging up and purchasing them right away," I replied.

"Okay. You've waited long enough. Normally, we don't allow families to travel before the passport is issued, but if you're willing to deal with the unknowns and possibly having to stay in India longer, go ahead and buy the tickets. In the meantime, I'll call Minal and we will put together a tentative itinerary for you. I'll email the embassy to make your visa appointment for next week, in hopes that her passport is issued before then. Once you purchase the tickets, please email me your flight info immediately. Minal will book the rooms at the hotel again and will need to know your arrival time," Lisa responded.

"AHHHH! I can't believe it!" my heart raced, "It's finally real! I'm going to get her, Lisa!" I started crying.

"Things are about to get crazy!" Lisa laughed, "I am so excited for you! Go get your tickets and don't forget to email me the information. I will call you back in two hours or so after Minal and I get everything worked out with the itinerary and appointments. I'll go over everything with you so that you know what to expect once you get Munni."

"Perfect! Thank you so much, Lisa. For everything!" I exclaimed.

I hung up the phone and called my travel agent. I purchased the tickets leaving the next day and arriving in India late in the evening on February 13. I couldn't believe it! I emailed Lisa my flight information and immediately attacked my task list. Laser focused, I worked like a machine getting all that needed to be accomplished before I left for India tomorrow afternoon - phone calls, laundry, packing, and lesson plans. It was on and I had never been so excited! Adrenaline pumped through my veins as I crossed another item off of the list. Nothing could stand in my way: my focus on Munni kept me energized and motivated.

* * * * *

I stepped out of the airport and took a deep breathe: the distinct earthy campfire smell of India filled my lungs. A smile spread across my face. In less than 24 hours I would have Munni in my arms! I got into the car and watched the nightlife of Hyderabad go by as we made our way to the hotel.

The driver pulled up to the familiar, elegant entrance. I hopped out of the car and immediately headed to the front desk. I felt like a gazelle, I was on cloud nine.

"Good evening," the hotel clerk greeted me, "are you checking in?"

"Yes! My name is Kristen Williams," I responded.

"Yes, ma'am. I have a message here for you from Ms. Minal," she said as she handed me a piece of paper.

I took the paper, unfolded it, and read the message:

> Another miracle, Munni's passport was issued late this afternoon. We will leave for the orphanage at 10 am. You will have your forever Valentine.

Tears filled my eyes as I silently thanked God for His incredible providence. "Did she already check-in?" I asked the clerk.

"No, ma'am. Her flight does not arrive until later. Here is your room key. Enjoy your stay," she said as she handed me the key and paperwork.

"Oh, I will!"

The porter stood behind me with the luggage cart and motioned to me towards the elevator. I could not stop smiling. Once in my room, I texted a few people to let them know I arrived safely and that Munni's passport had been issued. I took a quick shower to get rid of the travel grime and organized everything for the big day tomorrow. I knew sleep would be near impossible, but I prayed the jet lag would work to my advantage. I wanted to be as well rested as possible before getting Munni. I set my alarm and snuggled into bed. This was the last night I would go to sleep as a childless woman; our new life together started tomorrow. I drifted off to sleep thanking God for fulfilling all of His promises.

The next morning, I met Minal in the lobby and greeted her with a hug, "I can't believe the way everything happened!" I exclaimed.

"It's incredible," she replied, "but there has been a change. You need to fly to Delhi tonight instead of tomorrow. Lisa discovered that the Embassy will be closed on Monday due to President's Day and then the rest of the week due to the conference with CARA. We have to call and beg someone to meet you on Monday, regardless of the holiday. Because of Munni's age, she is required to get the TB test. That takes at least 48 hours before the doctor can read the results. You will start your medical tomorrow to allow enough time to get everything done before your flight leaves next Tuesday night. Lisa has already contacted Madhu. She will be your guide in Delhi."

"Wow. Never a dull moment," I laughed, "I should have known I wasn't finished with the drama!"

"When we get back from the orphanage, we will change the tickets for Delhi. Get ready for a whirlwind!" Minal emphasized.

"I'm ready! Nothing can steal my joy, knowing I finally have Munni with me," I declared as we both got into the car. My hands trembled with excitement; I was 15 minutes away from holding my daughter. I couldn't wait to take her out of that place and into my arms forever.

The car pulled up to the familiar iron gates that kept my daughter sequestered in her orphanage. I wanted to hit a fast forward button so I could be transported instantly to the lobby of the orphanage. Instead, the car ambled slowly down the long, dusty road to our destination; every minute driving felt like an eternity. The driver pulled over to the shade spot, I opened the my door before he put the car in park. I could no longer contain my excitement. Minal joined me and quickly walked inside the orphanage. Seated at the table where she conducted important affairs, Sanjeeta greeted us warmly.

I thought we would be instructed to wait in the lobby, but Sanjeeta called an ayah and told her to lead us back to Munni's room. I quickly turned on my iPad and began the video. This time, I was sure to record the moment. Minal and I followed the ayah down the long hallway, I stared at the black tile as I anxiously realized how close I was to seeing my daughter. My attention turned to a long line of children who stood single file. I watched in shock as the woman at the head of the line, seated in a chair, stuck the children with a needle. I assumed they were receiving vaccinations; however, the woman used the same needle for all of the children, reinserting it into the vial and poking the next child in line. My heart sank. How many times did that happen to Munni? What kind, if any, diseases and/or illnesses were spread through this practice? I was more thankful than ever that today was the last day of her existence in this place.

The ayah stopped at room number 6. I peered inside and smiled at the gaggle of giggling girls. They watched with wonder as I entered the room. Munni stood stoic with another ayah who brushed her short hair. Next, she poured a little bit of oil into her hands, rubbed them together, and ran it through Munni's hair. She brushed it back into place, a deep side part that provided coverage over one of the large burn scars. Munni stood as a statue as the ayah attended to her. She picked up a small paintbrush and dipped it into a color palette. She expertly applied a bindi on Munni's forehead. She finished the session by dusting her face with powder. Munni wore a beautiful, pink satin dress. She looked gorgeous. I smiled at her. She returned my smile with an icy stare, her black eyes sliced my heart. My fears materialized before me, she held a grudge and I didn't blame her. I knelt down next to her and gently put my hand on her back. Ever so slightly, she pulled away; her message clear: I had work to do in order to regain her trust.

The ayah attempted to force her to kiss me on the cheek. I immediately stood up and refused. I didn't want her to do anything that wasn't on her terms. I gave her space and turned my attention to the other little girls who were vying for my recognition. I wondered how many of them were matched with a family. It saddened me to think of them living their days in this place. I remembered several of them from my first visit and called them by name. They shrieked and ran behind one another, peaking out, laughing at the strange white woman standing in their room.

Finally, it was time to leave. The ayah handed me the photo book that I had sent with Heather. It looked worn, a hopeful sign that Munni had seen it. I took it and thanked her. I offered my hand to Munni. She looked at me, wavered, and then put her tiny hand in mine. I gently squeezed her hand and led her out of the room. We walked back down the long hallway despite my desire to sprint to the car. We stopped momentarily to say goodbye to Sanjeeta and then stepped out onto the front porch. I quickly put my sandals on and continued towards the vehicle. Munni never looked back. We got in the car and I motioned for Munni to sit on my lap, but she refused. Instead, she sat near the window, looking at life around her. I wondered what thoughts filled her mind. I put my hand on hers. She didn't move it. I hoped it was a positive sign of forgiveness.

The car pulled out and headed back to the administrative offices where more paperwork awaited me before we were free to leave. The driver parked next to the cement stairs and let us out. As we walked through the labyrinth of buildings, Munni let me hold her hand. We arrived back in the office of giant folder columns. I didn't recognize any of the women. Minal addressed an older lady. She walked to the wall and pulled out a file from the pillar. Still astounded at the seemingly lack of organization, it boggled my mind that anyone could ever find a file. Minal instructed Munni to pass out the chocolate candies we brought for the administrative team. She smiled when she opened to box and saw the chocolate. Minal told her to take one. She eagerly selected a piece of dark chocolate and popped it in her mouth. She turned to me and grinned. My heart melted, it gave me more hope for the restoration that needed to take place in our relationship.

While the woman gathered the papers, a news crew appeared at the entrance of the office. A conversation occurred between the news reporter and Minal. Minal signaled me to come out of the office. She told me they hoped to do a Valentine's Day story on adoption. Would I allow them to interview Munni and me? I told Minal that I would do whatever I could to advocate for adoption. She warned me not to state specifics about Munni's case; instead, keep it general. Once we agreed, the news team ushered us to a quiet place on the lawn, surrounded by beautiful flowers. I picked up Munni and held her as the reporter asked me questions. Halfway through the interview, the reality of my adoption being complete hit me like a ton of bricks. I started crying, gushing to the reporter about how much I loved Munni and how hard I fought for her. The reporter became misty-eyed and looked closely at my necklace. She instructed the cameraman to zoom in for a close-up. She adored the fact that I wore Munni's name around my neck; in her mind, it was a true sign of love and acceptance.

Thirty minutes later, Minal emerged from the office holding a file full of papers, "You're all set. Let's head back to the hotel!" she informed me as she handed me the folder. We walked back through the maze of buildings and got into the car. This time, Munni sat on my lap. I wrapped my arms around her and hugged her close to my chest. The driver pulled up to the massive iron gates for the very last time. I held my breath. I knew I wouldn't feel free until we passed through these gates. A small part of me worried that someone would chase after the car, informing us of a mistake in the paperwork. All I wanted to do was drive through the gates into freedom. The guard walked to the guardhouse and pushed the button. Nervously, I watched as the gigantic, barred doors slowly opened. Our driver pulled through and stopped at the busy road, waiting for an opportunity to enter the chaotic traffic. Finally, an open space materialized and the driver punched the gas pedal. The car accelerated and spun a hard left out of the orphanage. I turned and looked over my shoulder to see the iron gates locking shut behind us. A wave of relief washed over me. I squeezed Munni tightly as I looked out the windshield into the great future of our new life together. We were family. Both of us crowned with new titles: mother and daughter. From this point forward, nothing could change it.

Back at the hotel, Minal got right to work on changing our airline tickets. We had a few hours before we needed to leave for the airport, so I decided to give Munni a shower. I had the perfect dress picked out for her to wear. I bought it when I received NOC and saved it for this moment. Today was our first Valentine's Day together. On my last trip to Hyderabad for court, Minal informed me that Hyderabad is known as the city of pearls. She took me to an exquisite jeweler where I purchased for Munni her first pair of pearl and ruby bangles. I wrapped them in gorgeous paper and finished it with a beautiful bow. I wanted my first gift to her to be something she would never forget. After I applied lotion and helped her put on the new dress, I handed her my Valentine's gift. Her eyes filled with wonder she carefully unwrapped the package. She opened the box and saw the bangles. She looked at me with utter fascination and joy. I motioned for her to put them on. She quickly took them out of the box and slipped them onto her wrists; her entire face radiated with pure happiness. I hugged her and whispered in her ear, "Happy Valentine's Day, Munni! You're my forever Valentine, and I will love you for eternity!"

Even though I knew she didn't understand my words, I became certain she understood my heart. For the very first time, she hugged me back.

* * * * *

It had been a whirlwind since we arrived in Delhi. We rushed from one appointment to the next and then waited days for results and call backs. When I saw tiny blisters forming at the TB test site on Munni's arm only hours after receiving the shot on Friday, nervousness and worry filled my heart. The follow-up visit wasn't until Monday. I spent the entire weekend ruminating over the worst-case scenario. If she tested positive, we could potentially be stuck in India for months while she underwent treatment. She wouldn't be granted permission to enter the United States without it. I couldn't even allow my mind to grasp this potential outcome. Instead, I sent out a massive prayer request, pleading for healing and clear X-rays so we could leave Tuesday night on our original tickets. First thing Monday morning, we returned to the MedMax center where the doctor examined the TB test site on her arm. He confirmed my fears that she was reactive and ordered chest X-rays. I prayed silently through the entire procedure, hoping against hope, her reaction was due to the BCG vaccine that she received in the orphanage. I couldn't help but think back to the long line of children I saw, standing single file in her orphanage, all getting poked with the same dirty needle. I shuttered at the thought. After the X-rays were developed, the doctor put them up on the screen. He looked at them for what seemed like an eternity. I held my breath. Seemingly satisfied with what he saw, he took the X-rays off of the screen and shoved them in an envelope. The doctor signed a paper and handed me her medical packet. He looked me in the eyes. "Good luck," he told me as he extended his hand to mine.

"Thank you," I replied, a little off guard. It was a strange interaction.

Since I had managed to beg someone at the embassy to work on President's Day, it permitted us to start her visa interview right after we obtained the cleared X-rays from the doctor. It also guaranteed her visa would be ready by early Tuesday afternoon. We were cutting it close, but I prayed like crazy we would board the plane on time. All I wanted was to be in my own home with Munni. I was ready to start our lives together without the interruptions of interviews, doctor appointments, and immigration paperwork. The process had taken a toll and I wanted it to be over.

I woke early Tuesday morning because anxiety forbid any form of restful sleep. I looked at my phone and saw several missed calls from my neighbor and a friend who tag-teamed watching my dogs while I was gone. I saw ten messages on my text bubble. I quickly opened the first message to find out that Lola, my firecracker of a dog, had some sort of accident in the basement. From the messages and voicemail, it appeared she suffered from a neurological problem and the words "put down" were thrown around as possibilities. My stomach tightened and my heart sank. I did not want my dog to die while I was in India. I tip-toed into the bathroom and tried to call my neighbor and friend. Neither one answered. Panicked, I began my research on the words they used to describe her condition; my fears were not alleviated. I started to cry. Could this day start any worse? I called my friend Mer. She loved dogs as much as I did, and I knew she would understand the grief and anxiety that coursed through my body. Thankfully, she answered. We talked for twenty minutes, and somehow, she calmed me down. She prayed for me and urged me to focus on the tasks I needed to complete in order to leave on time. We hung up, and I prayed for the strength to get through the day. I prayed God would heal Lola, or at least, keep her alive until I got home. Then, I pushed it all into a compartment in my mind and closed the door.

Munni woke up and her arm appeared much worse. It definitely looked like a second-degree burn now. Thankful to have a clear X-ray from the doctor, I tried to push down the worry that tugged at my heart. Would her reaction be this bad if she wasn't truly positive? I thought about the strange way the doctor looked at me and how he wished me good luck. Something about it left me with an uneasy feeling. Did he know something more that he didn't reveal? In addition, her right eye looked like she contracted pink eye. This poor child. Her whole world just changed in every way possible and now she had a painful sore on her arm and an irritated eye. I hated that we weren't home, in the comfort of our house, where I could spoil her to her heart's content. I hugged and kissed her and asked for more prayers. Somehow, we needed to conquer this day and get on the plane headed for home.

* * * * *

We had started the visa interview Monday, right after we left the medical appointment with Munni's X-rays. I didn't know what to expect when we entered the embassy, or what kind of questions we would be asked in the interview, but never had I entered a building filled with such tension. Everyone standing in line wanted the same thing: a visa to enter the United States of America.

When the embassy worker finally called us for our turn, I thought I was going to pass out walking to her service window. My nerves were all over the place. She asked me several questions about my information, more questions about my agency, she asked if anyone demanded bribes, and then she requested Munni's medical paperwork. I offered the X-ray packet, but since it was too big for the service window slot, she told me to just keep it. She verified Munni's name and birth date, and she scribbled a few things down on a Post-it Note. She told me to come back the next day after 1:00 pm.

Late Tuesday morning, Munni and I waited in the lobby for our guide to take us back to the U.S. Embassy. Madhu pulled up to the hotel entrance and greeted us warmly. "How did you sleep, Kristen?" she asked.

"Not very well," I admitted. I spared her the details of the bad news I woke up to about my dog, Lola. I didn't want to say it out loud, because somehow, that made it worse.

"Tomorrow night, you will be sleeping in your own bed. Rest will find you there," she assured me.

I leaned back and looked out of the window. I couldn't wait to be in my house. I thought back to my flight home from Hyderabad, after I had to take Munni back to the orphanage. I met a businessman who had been living in India for years. He asked about my adoption process. I wasn't in the best frame of mind, having just left Munni behind, and knowing it would be at least two more months before I would see her again. He gave me sage advice that I never forgot. He told me, "If you don't have patience, India will give to you. If you have patience, India will take it from you." No truer words have been spoken about this process.

We arrived at the embassy and got out of the car. We passed through the security check and into the open-air lobby. On the way over, Madhu had prepared me for a long wait. She said to expect the visa issuance to take between 2-3 hours. She told us to continue inside while she used the restroom.

Munni and I entered the second building and followed the red painted line all the way down to the end of the room, to the area designated for U.S. citizens. We passed hundreds of Indians waiting in long lines. Heads turned as they watched a Caucasian woman and a little Indian girl walking by, hand in hand. I signed in and sat on the bench, settling in for the extended wait. Three minutes later, a woman called Munni's name. I jumped up and nearly sprinted the service window. Munni was right behind me.

"Hello. Are you Miss Williams?" the embassy worker asked.

"I am." I fumbled to get my passport out and slid it through the window slot.

The embassy lady took my passport and verified it was me. She smiled and then pushed a packet back through the slot. "Don't open that packet and make sure no one else opens that packet until you reach the immigration department at your port of entry in the United States." Then, she passed Munni's passport through the window slot. "Congratulations on your adoption!"

"Thank you." I said as tears ran down my face. "It's been a hard journey to get to this point," I could hardly speak, I was overcome with emotion. I wiped my tears and grabbed the packet and passport. I thanked her again, took Munni's hand, and headed for the door. Not even 15 minutes had passed since we entered the building. We walked to the open-air lobby. I saw Madhu. We made eye-contact and I immediately started to cry. She hastened her pace towards me with a worried look.

"Kristen, what's wrong?" she asked concerned.

"Nothing. Nothing at all. I have her visa!"

"You have her visa?" she asked stunned.

"Yes. I don't think we were in there 15 minutes. But, I have it. We are ready to go," I declared.

"You, my friend, have just set a record. I have never seen a visa issued this quickly. Congratulations!" Madhu said cheerily.

"Now, we just need to get on that plane. It's time for my daughter and me to go home. Together."

* * * * *

"Welcome to the United States of America," the officer greeted us as I carried Munni to the immigration desk.

After late night layovers and a long, 18 hour flight from Dubai to Dallas, I let out a giant sigh of relief, "You have no idea how great that sounds!"

"I bet," he responded as he continued processing our paperwork and the super secret adoption file marked 'DO NOT OPEN' given to me by the embassy. He asked me several questions about her adoption and then stamped our passports, handed them back to me, and wished us luck in our new life together.

I looked at my watch, the immigration process took longer than expected and I feared we were going to miss our last flight home. I picked up Munni, dressed in pajamas and flip flops from the cross-Atlantic flight, grabbed my rolling carry-on, and searched for a flight board so I could locate our departing gate. Staring at the screen, I couldn't find our flight. A friendly employee must have seen my confusion and asked if I needed help. I showed her my tickets and asked her if she thought we had enough time to get to the gate. She told me the gate and then assured me that if we ran, we could make it. That was all the encouragement I needed; I would have done anything to make that final flight home! I put Munni down, grabbed her hand, and started running. We had twenty minutes to make it to the gate that was a long way from where we were. We hustled through the crowds, dodging slow walkers, and running on the walking sidewalks. Munni grew tired easily so I carried her on my hip and continued my race to the finish. We were so close I could taste it. Finally, we arrived at the gate breathless, drenched in sweat, and exhausted. I put Munni down as I looked at the empty gate and used every ounce of self-control to not break down and cry. Another employee walked by and I pleaded for help, "I think we just missed our plane to Cincinnati. I don't know what to do next, I've been traveling for over 30 hours, and my mind is mush," I admitted.

The employee took my boarding pass and shook his head, "You're at the wrong gate. This is the international terminal. You were supposed to be in the domestic terminal, on the other side of the airport."

"You've got to be kidding me," I whined, "the lady at immigration told me to come to this gate. I just busted my butt running through the airport to get here. I can't believe this."

"I don't know why she told you this gate. I'm sorry. You're going to have to go back out through security to the ticket counter and see if they can get you on the next flight. Follow the signs to baggage claim. The ticket counters will be to the left of the baggage carousels," he said as he pointed to the sign directing me to the baggage claim, " but remember, once you get your tickets rescheduled, you'll have to take the tram back to the domestic terminal."

I thanked him for his assistance. Feeling deflated, I looked at Munni who looked at me with questioning eyes. I reached for her hand and told her, "On with the adventure!" I didn't want to upset her so I tried to remain positive. Her eye had worsened; I tried to keep her from rubbing it but it was obvious it bothered her. It seemed we would never make it home.

Delirious from lack of sleep and a full day of stress prior to boarding the plane in India, I managed to get us to the ticket counter. The lady got us on the next flight to Cincinnati two hours later. I made up mind to make the best of the situation. My clothes still wet with sweat, we walked slowly to the tram. Holding Munni's hand, I looked down and thanked God for her. She was the only thing that was important in this moment. Here she was, in the

United States with me. It was truly a miracle.

We wandered up to the tram, caught the next train, and sat down. Exhausted and overwhelmed, I couldn't wait to sleep in my own bed, next to Munni. I took out my phone and texted everyone that we missed our flight and gave them our new arrival time. A few minutes later, the tram stopped at our destination. I grabbed my carry-on, backpack, and held Munni's hand. We stepped off onto the platform, and I searched for signs directing me where to go. It seemed nothing was clearly marked. I didn't know if it was my lack of sleep, but I felt disoriented. We started walking towards the escalators when a couple approached me and said something I didn't understand. The woman kept trying to talk to me, but I couldn't comprehend what she was saying through her thick accent. Munni let go of my hand and darted. Distracted by the woman asking me questions, I quickly grabbed Munni's hand and pulled her back to me. Her husband remained a distant figure in my peripheral vision. Every time I looked in his direction, the woman asked me another question. After several attempts of trying to understand what she was asking, I gave up and told her I was sorry. I turned back towards the escalator with Munni and continued on our way.

We reached the bottom of the escalator, and my phone dinged in my back pocket. We stepped to the side, and I pulled it out to read the incoming messages. Everyone was super supportive and encouraged me to stay strong. I smiled and put my phone back in my pocket. I took Munni's hand and reached for my carry-on. Only, it wasn't there. I immediately panicked. Every important item I had from the trip was in my carry-on: all of Munni's adoption paperwork; documents I hadn't even had the chance to read, yet but Minal had somehow managed to copy from her orphanage file; my camera with the memory card; my lenses; and our clothes to change into before walking down the final terminal. I didn't care about the clothes, but the adoption paperwork and my camera would be fatal losses. Munni's birth certificate, the court order, my Hague certificate, all gone. Frantic, I looked around, but it was nowhere to be seen. I wracked my brain trying to remember the last time I had it. The up escalator was on the other side of the platform. I took Munni's hand and walked briskly to the other side and then sprinted up the escalator. We reached the platform and I retraced my steps. My carry-on never materialized. I paced back and forth on the platform. I know I had it when we left the tram. The last time I remembered having it was when the odd couple stopped me to talk. Did the woman distract me so her husband could take my bag? Did that really happen? I was so exhausted that I started to second guess myself. Did I remember to grab the carry-on when we departed the tram? Everything jumbled in my mind, I couldn't find a coherent thought. We went back down the escalator, I forced myself to remember every detail. Did I have it on the escalator? Was I holding the handle when my phone dinged? An exhausted haze clouded my memory.

I saw a policeman and ran to him. Munni stood next me, fear in her eyes. I quickly explained what happened. He asked me a few questions, my memory glazed over from stress and fatigue, I wasn't sure of anything anymore. He radioed for back up. Within minutes, we were surrounded by police wielding military style weapons. No longer able to hold it together, I broke down and sobbed. People stared at us with worried curiosity as they walked past us. Munni looked at me with questioning eyes, I tried to explain using pantomime and the color red, a word I knew she understood.

The clock ticked as our departure time grew near. The police filed a report and gave me names and departments to call once we arrived home. They informed me that they would review all of the security footage; however, the tram platform was the only place where security cameras were not installed. If the couple did in fact steal my bag, it would not be documented on film. In addition, they educated me on abandoned bags in airports; it was a rare occurrence and one that was handled swiftly and with the upmost caution. Ever since 9/11, any unattended bag was treated as a serious threat. Had I simply left my bag somewhere, they assured me it would have already been reported. I felt sick. It seemed my chances of ever getting my bag back were slim to none.

Finally, the time came to board our final flight home. A quick two hour flight and I would soon see the familiar faces of friends and family waiting for us; a sight I desperately needed. I quickly buckled Munni into her seat and motioned that I was going to the bathroom. I squeezed into the tiny airplane lavatory and locked the door. I looked in the mirror and willed myself to get it together. I splashed the gross airplane water onto my face, trying to erase the horrible events of the day. I patted my face dry with a paper towel and resolved myself to enjoy the rest of the flight. I had Munni. This was her homecoming, and I wasn't going to ruin it with sad tears. I took a deep breath, unlocked the door, and headed back to my seat. I sat down, turned to Munni, and kissed her on the top of her head. The flight attendant began the monotonous safety script as I held Munni's hand and closed my eyes. Almost home.

Two hours later, I looked out the window to see the beloved skyline of Cincinnati against the Ohio River. Excitement built in my chest. A smooth landing and welcome announcement from the flight attendant. I could hardly contain my giddiness. The flight crew opened the airplane door, and I practically knocked people down like bowling pins trying to get off the plane. Once out of the gate, I paused to send texts informing everyone that we landed and were headed towards the baggage claim. A final surge of adrenaline renewed my strength. I picked up Munni and practically skipped to the tram. With each stop, my heart beat faster. Finally, we reached the end of the tram line that would lead us to the baggage claim. I picked up Munni and began the long jaunt down the corridor, each step bringing us closer to home.

As we approached the end of the terminal, the crowd that looked like a blob from a distance, materialized into the smiling, joyful faces of those I loved most. Welcome home signs, balloons, and cheers greeted us and we crossed the line out of the terminal and into the waiting area. Strangers smiled as they watched the joyful occasion unfold. I walked with determined steps into the sea of love that awaited us. I melted into the arms of my loved ones and released grateful sobs that had been contained for way too long. We made it. We crossed the finish line. We were home.

CHAPTER 25
JULY, 2013

"Hello! It's good to see you two again!" the doctor greeted us as she walked into the exam room.

"Hi Mary! We decided to give you a break from seeing us so often," I joked with her. After months of medical procedures, surgeries, and mystery diagnoses, formalities disappeared and were replaced with first names. The entire spring felt like we lived at Children's Hospital. The parking attendants stopped asking for my validated tickets, they quickly realized we were regular patients and recognized us at each departure. A friendly wave became the substitution for the ticket extraction.

Mary looked over Munni's chart and noted her progress. Then, with tears in her eyes, she turned to me and confessed, "I didn't think this 6-month follow-up visit would happen. Munni was extremely ill, I was afraid she wasn't going to survive. If you hadn't brought her home when you did, she most certainly would have died. It's a miracle she's alive."

My mind flashed back to early spring. Two days after landing in Cincinnati, we boarded another plane to Florida for a quick trip so my parents could meet Munni during their winter getaway. During that stay, both Munni's arm and eye worsened. My sister and I thought she had pink eye, as it appeared glassy and angry red. The mark on her arm continued to eat away at the skin, widening with each day, and resembling a third-degree burn. She had an appointment scheduled with the International Adoption Clinic for the following Monday, but by Friday, I couldn't wait any longer and took her to the little clinic at Kroger's pharmacy to obtain some much needed erythromycin. However, the nurse practitioner had different plans. She took one look at Munni's eye and informed me that it wasn't pink eye, but whatever it was, she needed to be seen immediately. So much so, she called down to Children's Hospital emergency room to alert them we were on our way. Little did I realize that visit to the emergency room was the beginning of a nightmare that was about to become our reality.

Blood draws, labs, biopsies, MRIs, consultations with doctors from all over the country, and two surgeries later, they discovered that not only had the TB ravaged Munni's lungs, but it had spread systemically throughout her body, infecting various organs in its pathway of destruction. They found active TB in her lymph nodes and deep within her eye. The ophthalmologist who performed the biopsy was horrified at the depth which the TB penetrated her eye. It was so entrenched, he feared permanent damage and TB meningitis, a frightening diagnosis. Many times, I thought back to my strange interaction with the Indian doctor. I couldn't help but wonder, *Did he sign off on her paperwork to save her life?* In addition, her labs came back to reveal a host of unrelated serious complications that were never indicated anywhere in her Indian medical file. Everything that was discovered at Cincinnati Children's Hospital had been a complete and utter shock.

I remembered the fateful night snuggled up next to each other in our comfy bed, in the darkness, through broken English in a moment of trust, when Munni opened her Pandora's Box of horrors. In vivid detail no 6-year-old should know, she described abuse and torture so horrific that I lay silently while tears streamed down my face as Munni emptied the vault of hidden atrocities that plagued her childhood memories. It felt as if all of the oxygen had been sucked out of the room. I could barely breathe. I recalled how I prayed for the strength to listen, then how I waited for her to drift off to sleep. I could feel the acid in my stomach burn as soon as I heard her slumbered breathing. I quietly slid out of the bed, closed the bedroom door, and sprinted out of my house into my front garden where I vomited out all she had revealed to me. I thought about all of the scars that marked her frail, tiny frame and the mystery that once surrounded them in my mind. Now, I knew their horrendous story and how each one had carved its permanent existence on her body. On my knees, in the middle of the night, I sobbed in anguish for what my precious daughter had endured. Rage burned in my heart towards the one who inflicted these gruesome crimes against my daughter and I envisioned 5 minutes alone in a room with this individual; in my mind, I beat him to a bloody pulp and didn't stop even when his breathing did. In that moment, I repeated my vow: never again would anyone hurt my daughter. I'd die before I let that happen.

I recollected how through all of the trauma, medical complications, and baring of soul, our bond as mother and daughter grew intimate, deep, and completely cemented. Nothing could separate us. Our relationship and the attachment we formed was the most beautiful sweet that came from all of the bitter. Through the ashes of Munni's history, God created beauty in our love for one another. I marveled at the truth of His Word, and how He made good on His promise that He sets the lonely in families.[11] He took two separate, lonesome individuals who lived half a world away from each other and intricately wove our lives together. We were family. Nothing and no one would ever be able to take that away from us.

I looked at Munni sitting on the examination table, giggling at her Curious George stickers. As tears filled my eyes, I turned to Mary and agreed, "You're right. She's a miracle."

CHAPTER 26
AUGUST 5, 2013

Munni skipped to the car, her butterfly wings dancing with each hop. I smiled with joy watching as happiness radiated from her entire being. We soaked up the days of summer and spent as much time in nature as possible. We had spent the afternoon hiking around the reservoir. Tired, thirsty, and hungry, we decided to head home and cook dinner. I belted Munni in her booster seat and kissed the scar on her forehead. She grinned. She'd been home 5 months, but every day seemed like a new adventure and I still felt surprised that she was here with me. I turned on the car, put it in drive, and started down the bumpy road when my phone rang. I looked at the caller ID and saw Lisa's number. I immediately answered.

"Hello there!" her familiar voice greeted me.

"Hey! How are you?" I asked.

"I'm wonderful. Busy, but wonderful," she replied. "It's been several weeks since we last spoke, and I wondered if you were still at peace with your final decision about Africa and moving forward with India?"

"Ugh, Lisa," I groaned. "That was a difficult decision. When I found out about all of the corruption and unethical practices my agency was involved in with the Congo adoption program, I knew I couldn't move forward with them."

"I know that was a painful decision for you. You'd been waiting for your baby boy for so long," Lisa empathized.

"It was horrible. But, I knew I couldn't adopt a child in good conscience knowing what I knew. When the whistleblowers started their new agency and contacted me about the Nigeria program, I was excited. However, I also felt God nudging me to return to India. The thought of three kids, well, I wasn't sure the direction God wanted me to pursue."

"It's never cut and dry, is it?" she pondered.

"No, it's not. You know I had been praying for clarity," I reminded her.

"And I was praying with you, hoping God would make it crystal clear and fill your spirit with peace," she told me.

"They emailed me two weeks ago to tell me the Nigeria program is a pilot program and they could put me on the wait list, but the soonest I could be accepted into the program would be next May."

"That's a long wait," Lisa noted.

"Too long. I really felt that was an answer to my prayer, so I officially closed the door on Africa, and I still have total and complete peace about that decision. In regards to your question, I'm ready to look for Munni's baby sister in India!" I exclaimed.

"Oh, Kristen, I'm thrilled God led you back to India."

"The funny thing is, the moment I declined a spot on the waitlist, peace flooded my heart. During Munni's adoption, I never dreamed I'd willingly put myself through another grueling process. Just the thought of it made my stomach hurt. Now, I can't wait. I know that's from the Lord!" I laughed.

"I have to confess, there's another reason I called," Lisa informed me.

"Okay. I'm nervous," I admitted.

Lisa laughed, "Oh, it's nothing to be nervous about. But I wanted to know where your heart was before I proceeded. I found a little girl, and as soon as I saw her face, I immediately thought of you and Munni."

"Wait, are you serious?"

"I am. I think she's perfect for your family," Lisa affirmed.

"Oh my goodness, Lisa. I need details. This is crazy! But, a great crazy."

Lisa chuckled, "I know. The Lord works in mysterious ways. When I saw this little baby, I just knew in my heart I had to call you."

"How old is she? What information do you have about her?" I eagerly questioned as my heart raced with excitement.

"She's 20-months, and she's perfectly healthy. You know what the situation with baby girls is like in India, especially in rural places, right?"

"Yes, I do. And it breaks my heart," I responded.

Lisa sighed, "When she was a newborn, she was abandoned near a garbage pile. Fortunately, somebody found her, but before they did, the animals chewed off her little nose," Lisa said gently.

I gasped in shock as I tried to process what this innocent baby endured. No one to protect her, no one to comfort her. My heart broke and I felt sick at the world in which we live.

"It's horrible," Lisa sympathized. "However, her face is so sweet. She has the most beautiful, big, black eyes you've ever seen."

"You're killing me, Lisa. I'm still twenty minutes from my house, driving home from the park. Can you email me her picture?"

"Of course! I want to hear your reaction when you see her. I think she's gorgeous. Minal called the orphanage and they told her that she's a completely healthy child, except for her nose. The doctors in India recommended reconstructive surgery when she's 7-years-old," Lisa informed me.

"This is torturous. I can't wait to see her picture!"

"You've done such a wonderful job with Munni and handling her facial scars. When I saw this little baby, there wasn't a doubt in my mind that she belongs with you," Lisa stated.

My heart pulsed with excitement. I couldn't get to my house fast enough. Was this my daughter? Was this baby going to be Munni's little sister? My thoughts whirled while Lisa continued to share information from the little girl's file. Finally, I parked in our driveway and quickly helped Munni out of the car. I hurried to my front door, unlocked it, and rushed to my computer. Munni followed right behind me. It seemed like an eternity for my computer to pull up my email. I opened my inbox and found Lisa's email right away. I looked at Munni and told her, "This might be your little sister!"

"Did her picture attach?" Lisa asked me.

"Yep, I'm just about to open it," I answered as I clicked on the email. Within seconds, staring back at me from the screen, was the most beautiful, tiny baby I had ever seen. Her giant, round eyes held a steady gaze. She couldn't have been more than a few months old in this picture. Thin, black hair barely covered her head. She wore a red sweater that looked like it had Christmas decorations sewn onto it. Where her nose should have been, revealed a teeny, tiny hole in the shape of an upside down heart. Joy permeated my entire being. I looked at Munni, who squealed and clapped her hands together. Tears rolled down my cheeks as love for this baby already began to grow in my heart. "Lisa! She's perfect!"

Giggling, Lisa agreed, "Didn't I tell you? She's beyond adorable."

"Do you know if she's still available? I'm afraid to get my hopes up in case she's already matched with a family and CARA hasn't removed her from CARINGS yet." I worried, thinking back to when Munni was still listed long after being matched with me.

"I already checked. She's not matched. If you're ready, she's available," Lisa informed me.

I smiled as I stared at her baby picture, my new daughter. I turned to Munni who hadn't stopped grinning while looking at the photo. In that moment, there wasn't a shadow of a doubt in my mind: this baby was ours. Lisa was right, she was meant to be in our family. I looked at my computer screen again and focused on the sweet face gazing back at me. My heart beat loudly in my chest and excitement spilled out into tears. I turned to Munni and made my bold declaration, "That's your baby sister!"

REFERENCES:

CHAPTER 1
1. Matthew 25:40

CHAPTER 6
2. Handel, George Frideric. "Every Valley Shall Be Exalted." Messiah (1741)

CHAPTER 14
3. Genesis 18:14

CHAPTER 17
4. Genesis 18:14

CHAPTER 18
5. John 14:14
6. James 1:27
7. Isaiah 55:8-9

CHAPTER 19
8. Genesis 18:14

CHAPTER 22
9. Isaiah 55:8

CHAPTER 23
10. Genesis 18:14

CHAPTER 25
11. Psalm 68:6